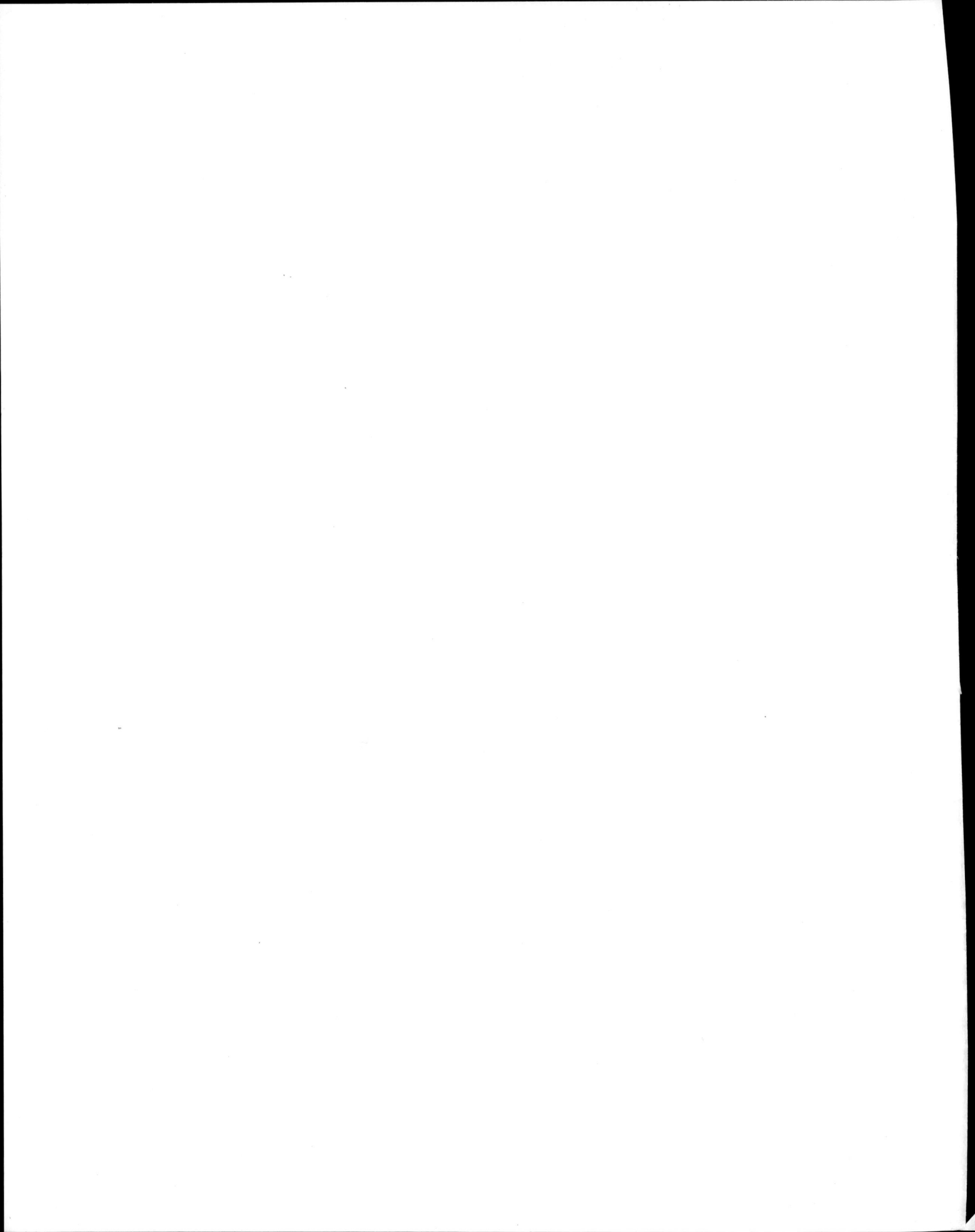

INDIAN ARCHITECTURE

ISLAMIC PERIOD
1192–1857

Indian Architecture

ISLAMIC PERIOD
1192–1857

Text and Photographs
Dr. Surendra Sahai

PRAKASH BOOKS

Acknowledgements

Completion of a manuscript is always followed
by a feeling of relief and satisfaction. When I
started work on this project I felt a little daunted
by the immense task of studying Islamic
monuments in India, beginning with the
founding of the Delhi Sultanate in 1192. My
fascination for the art and architecture of
medieval India inspired me and kept me engaged
on the work. In this task I have been greatly
helped by Prof. K.M.Shrimali, Professor of
History, Delhi University, who encouraged me by
offering valuable suggestions for improvement
of the script. He also read the final script.
Without his help, my task would have been very
difficult. I also wish to thank my colleagues-
Mr. Man Mohan Rai, Dr.J.P. Srivastava, Dr.R.P.
Bahuguna and Dr. Vipul Singh for their advice
and suggestions. And to my wife Mrs. Meenakshi
Sahai, I owe special thanks for her patience.

I am specially thankful to Mr. Ashwani
Sabharwal, my publisher, for his constant
encouragement while I was writing this book
and for allowing me all the time I required for it.

INDIAN ARCHITECTURE
ISLAMIC PERIOD

First published by Prakash Books India (P) Ltd.
1 Ansari Road, Daryaganj
New Delhi 110002
Email: sales@prakashbooks.com
Phone: +91 11 2324 3050/51/52
Fax: +91 11 2324 6975

© Prakash Books India (P) Ltd. 2004

Illustrations & Book Design by Supriya Sahai

ISBN 81-7234-057-5

Pictures on pages 44-49 and 96-97 by
Shahid A Makhfi, New Delhi.
Printed & Bound at Ajanta Offset, New Delhi.

INDIAN ARCHITECTURE
ISLAMIC PERIOD

INTRODUCTION

The Muslim conquest over northern India in 1192, was an epoch-making event. The Rajput forces led by Prithvi Raj Chauhan of Ajmer were annihilated at Tarain, near Delhi in their second encounter with the armies of Muhammad Ghori, the Turkish-Afghan chief of Ghor, the area between Ghazni and Herat in Afghanistan. The entire northern India was governed by Qutbuddin Aibak, Ghori's slave general. The two earlier Muslim invasions had a short-lived effect on India's political life. In 711, Debal in Sind was conquered by Muhammad Bin Qasim. It introduced Islam to India but never consolidated the small territorial gains into a firmly established kingdom. It was only in the early 11th century that northern India experienced the first shock of Muslim forces when the Turkish Ghaznavids from Afghanistan, led by Mahmud Ghazni, invaded the country lying between Gujarat and Varanasi, plundered at will and ransacked temples for hidden treasures. Ghazni went back to Afghanistan and ruled over portions of Punjab from Lahore. Muhammad Ghori was a soldier of a different mettle with immense capacity to organise campaigns and determination to fight.

The mighty Rajputs, indolent and faction-ridden, vein about their military prowess, great numbers and elephants, lost predictably to the agile cavalry of the Ghori. Almost all the Rajput strongholds Ajmer, Kannauj, Kalinjar, Gwalior etc. succumbed to the force of Qutbuddin Aibak. The eastern India yielded itself to Ikhtiyaruddin Muhammad Khilji, another commander of Muhammad Ghori.

Qutbuddin Aibak ruled on behalf of Ghori and founded the rule of the Slave dynasty. Most of Ghori's generals were purchased as slaves in open market. It was a common practice. Many of these slaves belonged to noble families and were given rigorous military training. No stigma was attached to their upbringing and status, and some of these slaves rose to great eminence as commanders of the army and administrators. This was the foundation of the Delhi Sultanate in 1192.

Architects of the Delhi Sultanate were heirs to a rich architectural tradition, mature and beautiful. The whirlwind military campaigns of the Umayyads, the earliest dynasty of Arab caliphs, brought most of the neighbouring territories under the sway of Islam. Soon after the death of the Prophet in 632 the Byzantine empire lost the east Mediterranean sector to the Umayyads. The Sassanian Empire succumbed entirely to the new powers. Damascus fell in 635, Jerusalem in 638, Egypt in 640-41 followed by Iran falling bit by bit. Some of the greatest mosques of the Islamic world were constructed immediately: the Great Mosque of Kufa in 638, the Dome of the Rock in Jerusalem in 691, the Great Mosque of Damascus 705-15, the Great Mosque of Kairawan in 836-62, Mosque of Ibn Tulun, during 886-

79 and the Mosque of al-Hakim during 990-1013 in Cairo. The aesthetic and architectural traditions of these great centres, the Hellenistic and Roman traditions and the Persian influence helped evolve the architectural idiom of the Islamic world during the seventh and eighth centuries. The first requirement of Islam was the construction of a mosque where the believers could assemble for prayers and community gatherings. The house of the Prophet Muhammad in Medina served as the prototype of the basic hypostyle mosque architecture. The grand courtyard, enclosed by a mudwall, had colonnades of palm trunks supporting a flat roof at the southern end and a smaller roofed area at the northern end. Entrance gates stood on the north, west and eastern walls. The rectangular courtyard with a hypostyle hall on the Qibla side became the ideal mosque structure. The direction of prayer was revealed to the Prophet in a revelation in 624. Henceward Mecca was to be his Qibla. He used a high seat over three steps as mimbar to address gatherings.

The early examples of architecture emphasised a few basic requirements: the *mihrab* (niche on the qiblawall) indicating the direction to be faced, positioned at the point where the Qibla axis meets the far wall of the mosque: maqsura-area near the *miharb* usually canopied and reserved for the royalty; mimbar-the pulpit to the right of the *mihrab*, raised on a few steps from where the Imam led the prayers; the ablution tank in the courtyard for ritualistic cleansing before the prayers. The Prophet's Abyssinan attendant Bilal used to climb up a high spot to give the call to prayer a functional requirement leading to the ultimate erection of the minaret or the minar.

The Umayyads made confident political statements through the mosque structures built over sites originally held by the Christians. The Dome of the Rock in Jerusalem, the first monumental mosque of Islam, was built over the spot where once stood the temple of Solomon, destroyed in 70. The rock is associated with the Creation itself. From here, the Muslims believe, the Prophet ascended to Seven Heavens in the course of his miraculous Night Journey. The architectural style of the Dome reflects Christian martyria. The Great Mosque at Damascus was built at the site of the church of St. John the Baptist. The entire Christian site was purchased, dismantled and rebuilt as a mosque. All through there is an uninhibited use of the column and capital; pointed arch and dome; rib and vault-architectural elements derived from the non-Islamic culture around Syria. The deep-rooted Hellenism and receptiveness to new ideas, forms and creativity were all too manifest in the earlier Islamic architecture.

Baghdad, capital of the Abbasid caliphs, showed a greater proclivity towards Iranian culture and architecture. The stray examples of figural sculpture seen on religious and secular buildings of the Umayyad period disappear almost completely, now replaced by geometrical designs, the classical foliate ornament becomes increasingly abstract and denaturalised. Geometrical formations form the basis of a remarkable orderliness in Islamic architectural, ultimately evolving into intriguing and unending extensions as essential element of surface ornament.

During the tenth and 11th centuries, the Saljuqs, Turkish nomads recently converted to Islam, ran through the greater part of the Arab caliphate to control Iraq, parts of Syria and Iran and westward to Anatolia. The Saljuqs built madarsas (school for religious instruction) to strengthen orthodoxy in Islam. They gave a classic architectural form to the four-iwan plan with a

above: Plan of the Dome of the Rock.
facing page: Dome of the Rock, Jerusalem, 691.

courtyard and a monumental domed chamber. The pishtaq acquires a grand appearance. Now gallery zones, engaged corner columns and double dome were added to the square domed chamber of the basic architectural form of the mausolea. The style of the minaret under Iranian influence acquires a grand and ornamental form. The earlier minarets had a square shape in Syria, Spain and North Africa. In Samarra and Fustat, the minaret had a spiral form. The tapering cylindrical form, including the inbuilt single or double staircases, corbelled balconies, three-tiered elevation, use of flanges and engaged columns are the typical Saljuq features. The double minaret flanking the iwan is yet another feature of the Saljuq architecture which went on to appear with regular frequency all over the Islamic world. Later on the Ottomans increased the number of minarets at mosques to five or six. When Sultan Ahmad I provided six minarets at his mosque in Jerusalem, the number of minarets at the Mecca mosque had to be raised to seven to maintain its prestigious position as the most sacred mosque of Islam. Muqarnas or honeycomb vaulting designed for filling the voids of the arched structure and used as mouldings and covering curved surfaces now becomes a part of the Islamic ornament.

The Saljuq architecture employs marble inlays to create wall surfaces of a rich and variegated colour schemes. The great Saljuq empire was shattered by the Mongol invasions in the 13th century when many Saljuq artisans and master builders moved to the greener pastures on the eastern horizons of the Islamic world.

The most characteristic form of Islamic ornament is calligraphy. Verses in Arabic from the Quran are used for their religious, symbolic and decorative values. Inscribed in stone or stucco, around the mihrab, below the dome, frame of the iwan and pishtaq, and as bands running around the circular shaft of the minaret, these calligraphed verses are not meant to be read; they are there in affirmation of the Faith. The calligraphic ornament replaces figural sculpture and creates an awareness of values beyond the ken of materialism.

The true character of Islamic architecture reveals itself not through the mass of structural forms but through the "hidden architecture", which is, as Ernst J. Grube (Professor of Islamic Art, Universities of Venice and Padua) explains; "architecture that truly exists, not when seen as monument or symbols visible to all and from all sides, but only when entered, penetrated and experienced from within… hidden architecture may be considered the main and dominant form of truly Islamic architecture". What makes the mosque the abode of Allah, the one God, is not dome, iwan, or the grand courtyard but the whole atmosphere of spiritual serenity and divine presence where you realise the truth: "The One remains, the many change and pass; Heaven's light forever shines, Earth's shadows fly", as P.B. Shelley sums up the essence of all religions in the world.

The exterior of buildings-mosques, tombs or palaces appears unpretentious in decoration. The interiors, however, are a dazzling world of exquisite ornament which creates the impression of weightlessness and unlimited space through

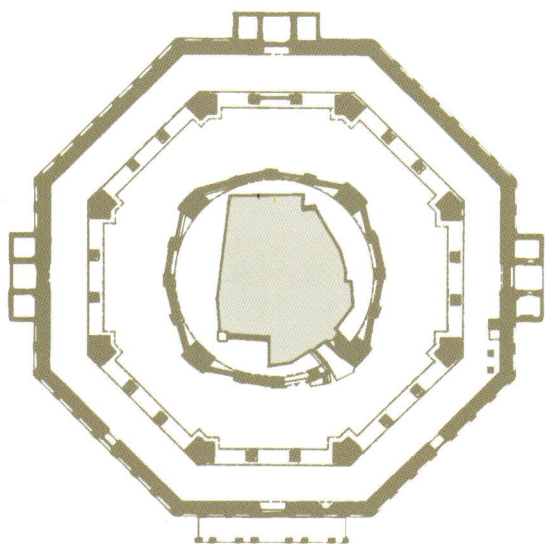

mosaics and tiles, fenestrations, vaulting, floral and geometrical arabesque, repetition of architectural elements like arches, bays, columns, passages, cupolas and doorways. Domes, squinch arches, stalactite pendentives or muqarnas create the illusion of extended space. Water channels, running through the palace areas, mosques and gardens create the same impression of uncircumscribed space besides underlining the fascination for the Garden of Paradise, heaven of flowers and fertility. The Islamic architect created this paradise through floral patterns and vegetal scolls covering both internal walls, carpets, tents and costumes. The Islamic ornament is the world's most colourful ornament, seeking perhaps, a psychological compensation for the drabness of the desert and a harsh landscape signally wanting in charms supplied by water and the enchanting spring.

The Islamic architecture, spanning land between Spain and India, the Steppes and Arabia is remarkable for its homogenous character. The people of different lands bound each to each with the single thread of monotheistic belief and brotherhood required only some basic architectural forms where they could meet for prayer. The four-iwan courtyard plan has a great adaptability to function as mosque, tomb, madarsa, palace or caravanserai. It has a universal form, nearly ubiquitous in Islamic architecture. The forms of ornament also are not limited to any particular form of architecture. Abstract designs vegetal bands, geometrical patterns appear on mosques as well as tombs and minarets. The ingeniously calligraphed verses from the Quran not only have a spiritual significance but also immense value as ornament. Added to this all-purpose adaptability of the Islamic architecture is another unique feature-the structural plan can be extended in any direction without affecting its original purpose, particularly seen on secular architecture-forts, palaces, caravanserais and markets etc.

Amongst the various architectural elements, it is the arch, which lends itself admirably to diverse architectural and decorative effects. It appears as a modest entrance, an impressive iwan, a grand pishtaq, a mihrab in the sanctuary, as niche on the wall, as squinch and pendentive at the corners forming the zone of transition below the dome, in diminutive forms in mere continuous repetition or as blind niches. The arch appears indispensable to the various forms in Islamic architecture.

A hadith informs us on the Prophet's views on architecture: "The most unprofitable thing which eats up the wealth of a believer is building". Perhaps it overlooked man's inner urge to express himself through architecture. Soon after the Prophet's death in 632, mosque structures sprang up in all corners of the Islamic world, not only to provide a place for worship and congregations but also to establish the political power of the caliphate and the presence and power of Islam. But the most conspicuous architectural form belonged to the tomb commemorating the dead, though not encouraged by Islam. The development of funerary architecture became a widespread phenomenon, no doubt inspired by a desire to venerate saints and holy men and princely vanity.

Veneration of the tombs of the Shia saints and holy men led to the building of a great number of tombs during the ninth and tenth centuries. The ruling princes built their tombs on a more ambitious scale. Biblical persons, relations of the Prophet, scholars and fighters for the Faith had tombs built for them. Egypt and Central Asia had a large number of tombs in the tenth and 11th centuries. Aswan had nearly 50 examples of early tomb structures built in a cluster. Other examples of early tomb structures are found in Cairo, Fez, Ravy (near Tehran) and Samarkand. The smaller tombs had a circular form with a conical or pyramidal roof and the more ambitious tombs had a square structure crowned with a circular dome, decorated with brick and tiles or in stucco. The building of tombs on a monumental scale appeared in its most perfect and glorious form under the Mughals in India owing considerably to inspiration from tomb architecture in Iran in the 15th and 16th centuries.

The present book deals with the architecture, which makes an aesthetic statement of the culture nurtured by Islam and which is what distinguishes it from other non-Islamic architectural

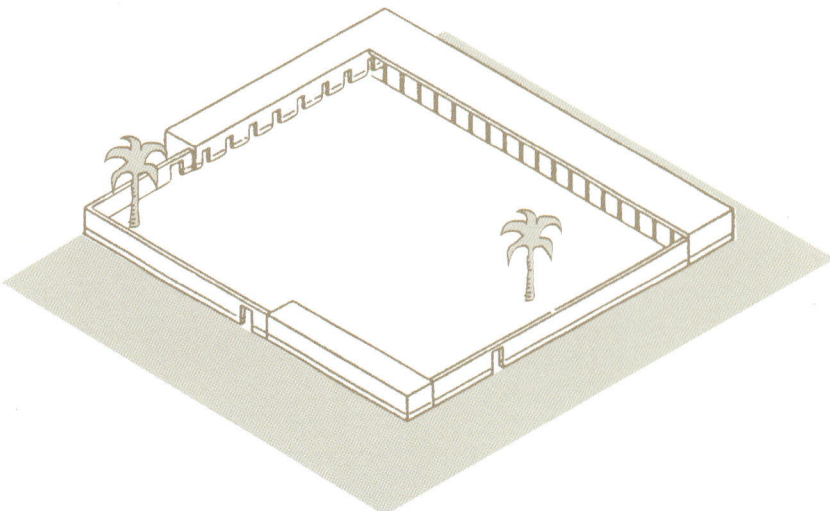

Above (left). House of the Prophet Muhammad. Medina, 624, model for many a mosque built later.   *Above (right). Plan of the Mosque of the Prophet Medina, 707-9.*

creations. Undeniably, the architecture of the mosque, madarsa and tomb articulates the religious, cultural and political phenomenon, which owes its existence to Islam. Islamic architecture is the architecture produced for the followers of the Prophet. More than anything else, it fosters the Islamic religion and culture.

Looking at the Islamic architecture from a different viewpoint K.M.Shrimali, Professor of History, Delhi University questions the use of the term 'Indo-Islamic' (in the Indian context). He reads in it "the imperialist objective of fomenting a religious divide in India", perpetuated by the European scholars, British administrator-cum-historians, art critics, etc. Their use of this "religion-centered vocabulary" is found to be of little use in describing distinctively religious structures in Europe for which purpose the terms used are invariably "functional, region-specific or people-specific. Thus we get to read about 'Roman' (not pagan or Christian) arch, Gothic or Roman lettering (contrast these with Islamic calligraphy), Doric or Ionic columns. We do not use Catholic spire, Protestant steeple or a Methodist vault. Why do we then use 'Hindu architrave' and 'Islamic dome'?" The use of the term Indo-Islamic architecture "to characterise the fusion of the two different cultural streams is rather jarring. A combination of unrelated components (geographical region and religion in this context) is a contrived formulation", according to Shrimali.

The early historians of architecture in the Indian sub-continent perhaps found it easier to distinguish, by using the term 'Indo-Islamic, the architecture of the Delhi Sultanate, its regional variations, and of the Mughals from the architecture preceding the founding of the Sultanate in 1192. No other term, however, so well covers various aspects or the architecture created by followers of the Islam, irrespective of long distances separating Spain and India, Anatolia and Arabia. It is the faith in the Prophet and Islam which holds them together and inspires their architecture.

Tomb of the Samanids, Bukhara, c. 943

1
THE EARLY TURKISH SULTANS & THE KHILJIS

Qutbuddin Aibak was one of the Turkish slaves of Muhammad Ghori appointed governor of the newly won territories in the northern India in 1192, Aibak assumed independent charge as the Sultan of Delhi in 1206 following the death of Ghori. The slaves generally belonged to a good background. The intelligent and hardworking slaves often went on to achieve a high status and role in administration. If they lacked royal blood, they attained royalty in their own right justifying the confidence of their master. Aibak rose to eminence by sheer hard work and dedication to the task assigned to him. In the beginning he stayed at Lahore. Delhi became the nucleus of the Sultanate only after Iltutmish ascended the throne in 1210 in the Qila Rai Pithora of Prithvi Raj Chauhan, the illustrious Rajput king, defeated and killed by Ghori after the decisive second battle at Tarain in 1192. This was known as Dihli-I-Kuhna or old Delhi of the Sultanate.

Quite understandably, the Quwwat-ul-Islam (might of Islam) Masjid at the heart of the Rajput fort, was the first structure built by Aibak to herald his political supremacy and the religion of the conquerors. An inscription on the inner lintel of the eastern gateway to the mosque contains the relevant details: "This fort was conquered and this Jami Masjid was built in the year 587 (1191-92) by the Amir, the great and glorious commander of the army, Qutbu-d-daulat-wa-d-din, the Amir'ul-Umara Aibak Sultani, may God strengthen his helpers. The materials of 27 temples, on each of which 2,000,000 Deliwals had been spent, were used in the construction of this mosque. May God the great and glorious have mercy on him who should pray for the faith of the good builder." The Persian inscription on the northern gateway to the mosque records another important information: "In the year 592 (1195), this building was erected by the high order of the exalted Sultan Muizu'd-dunya-wa-d-din Muhammad-bin-Sam, the helper of the Prince of the faithful." Perhaps, the mosque was completed in 1195. Whereas, the major portion of the existing temple was destroyed, the plinth of the original structure was retained and enlarged to form a stylobate large enough to accommodate construction of the mosque. Pillars, richly carved with Hindu sculptural motifs, were freely used, mostly placed one upon another to obtain the required height. Corridors on the east, north and south sides were thus built by reassembling stones from the demolished structures. The sanctuary, retaining sculptured pillars

left. Pillars from pre-Muslim ruins at the Qutb Minar mosque, Delhi.

undisturbed, was covered by shallow domed ceilings. A mihrab on the western wall indicated the direction of Mecca. Clerestories on the north-east and south-east corners of the corridors were provided for the ladies, reached through narrow stairs built within the thick outer walls. The basic structure of the mosque was completed in a hurry. To Aibak's discerning eye, however, the mosque was far from being complete: it looked merely an archaeological miscellany.

Soon after his return from Ghazni in 1199, Aibak ordered construction of an arch screen in front of the sanctuary, following example of the maqsura (screen), built in bricks, separating the sanctuary from the courtyard at the Prophet's Mosque in Medina. This five-arched screen contained a grand high central arch flanked by two smaller arches on either side, repeated in a similarly built smaller arches over them. Nine arches appeared to form a magnificent architectural achievement at this early stage of the Sultanate. The surface of these arches is covered with Quranic verses in bold Naskhi letters along with bands of foliage, its serpentine tendrils sculptured in an amazing rhythmic flow. The spiral forms of the foliage and other designs overwhelm the inscriptions. The artisans, who carried out the new assignment, had perhaps worked on the demolished temples a decade or two before this. They used all their hereditary skill with chisel and hammer on the sculptural splendour of the screens without understanding the purpose or significance of the inscriptions.

The arches were still principally corbelled and not on principles of the radiating voussoirs which form the core of the true Islamic arch. Thus the slight ogee (S) shape at the apex of the arch looked beautiful but incongruous in its present setting. The Buddhist chaitya windows, with their curved arches, still inspired the artisans and stoneworkers. The arch screen at the first great congregational mosque of the Delhi Sultanate remains an independent and splendid architectural creation in the history of the Islamic architecture in India.

The Quwwat-ul-Islam Masjid was still far from being completed. Iltutmish decided to double the size of its enclosure to accommodate the increasing Muslim population. To this end, he extended the original screen of arches on the north and south sides in alignment with the line of Aibak's arches. The mosque corridors were also extended on the east, north and south sides, pierced by suitable lofty gateways. Only a portion of the southern gateway has survived. The stone columns used on the extensions are also not as elaborately sculptured as at Aibak's original structure. The change in the style of decoration, from Aibak to Iltutmish, appears in the latter's insistence on chaste geometrical arabesque and calligraphic design rescued from the proliferating bands of convoluting foliage. In fact, Iltutmish achieved a complete denaturalisation of forms. Combination of the square Kufic and the elaborately woven Tughra characters appears a marked improvement on the mixed effect of ornamentation on Aibak's arhces. The ogee at the apex of the arches is a much subdued and straightened line, more acceptable to the purist. A small but new decorative device appears at these arches-the mutakha columns set in the recessed angles of the

pier jambs of the screen. The artisans had still to forget some of their patiently learnt devices of sculptural ornamentation.

Qutbuddin Aibak could not complete the great triumphal tower-the Qutb Minar. At the time of his death in 1210 only the first storey of the minar was ready. Iltutmish resumed work on the minar and added three more storeys to it, topped by a cupola. The Qutb Minar, completed in 1215 has remained one of the greatest architectural achievements of Islamic architecture in India. According to Percy Brown, renowned historian of architecture, "there is nothing like it in the whole range of Islamic art".

The first three storeys of the minar are differently designed. The first has wedge-shaped flanges alternating with rounded flutes. The second has only rounded projections and the third is star-shaped. The present fourth and fifth storeys, work of Firoz Shah Tughlaq, are circular, making sumptuous use of white marble in preference to the red sandstone used on the lower storeys. Lightning struck the minar in 1368 and Firoz, repairing the fourth damaged storey, replaced it with the two storeys in marble.

The most remarkable feature of ornamentation on the minar is the horizontal bands of inscriptions in Naskh and Kufic characters. The balconies on the tapering exterior show most exquisitely sculptured projections. The stalactite bracketing, an ingenious method of supporting the weight of projecting balconies, is here represented by a cluster of miniature arches or small alcoves with brackets in between, an attempt to reproduce the true geometrical stalactite effect but obviously influenced by the cusped tracery in the indigenous designs of temple ceilings. The stalactite treatment comes from the Egyptian 'george' which is an ornamental cornice of roll and hollow mouldings, crowning massive walls called 'muqarnas' in Arabic, the stalactite has a notable element of fantasy, a pile of blind arches, one above the other on their periphery. A small doorway on the northern side provides entrances to the in-built flight of 379 steps to the top at 72.3m. The doorway has an inscriptional panel below a row of Kanjuras (merlons) viewed from a little distance. The Qutb Minar appears in its full splendour, a tribute to the Indian mason's unexcelled creative genius and the admirable timelessness of his handiwork.

The numerous inscriptions on the Qutb provide epigraphically evidence of immense historical value. The inscriptions on the first storey eulogise Muhammad bin Sam (Ghori) and mention Aibak as 'The Amir, the Commander, the Glorious, the Great'. It also records 'imarat minarah mubarik hazarat Sultan-al Duniya wa-aldin Mahroom'. A much damaged inscription on the first storey mentions "al minarah Fazl Abul Maali boondad…' (of this minar was Fazl Abul Maali). He was perhaps the chief architect of Aibak's works since his name also appears on one of the piers of the mosque.

The Turks were well acquainted with the square towers as adjunct of the mosque at Qasrul Banat, Sergius, Bacchus and St. George in Sama. The spiral minaret at the Great Mosque at Samarra, near Baghdad, was also a famous tower, independent of the mosque. But the two great minarets of Jam and Siah Posh in

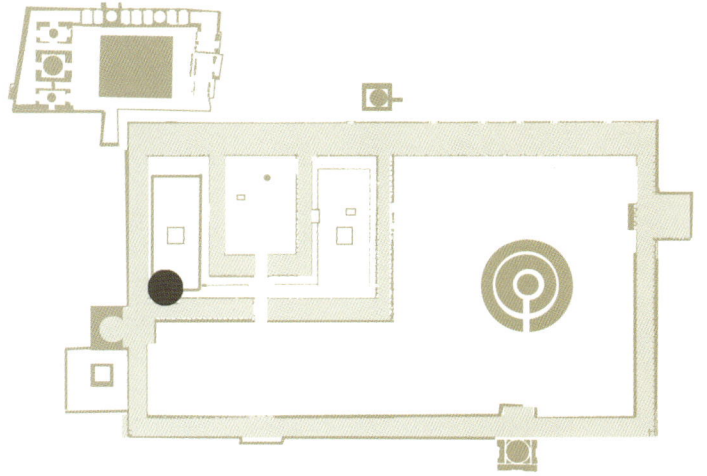

left. Tomb of Iltutmish at the Qutb.

above. Plan of the Qutb complex.

below. Quwwat-ul-Islam Mosque at the Qutb.

Afghanistan considerably influenced the design and concept of the Qutb Minar. Ghiyasuddin, Muhammad Ghori's brother, built the Jam minaret in celebration of his victory over the land dominated by the Hebrews. It is a brick structure on an octagonal base, with a height of nearly 18m divided into three storeys. There are balconies projected on corbelled masonry brackets. The minaret is crowned by a lantern pavilion. A spiral staircase winds up around the central shaft leading to the top. Ample surface decoration in Kufic and Naskh characters, wine-leaf roundels in stucco and blue tile faience are essentially Islamic.

The Siah Posh minar, built in the late ninth or early tenth century in the Nimroz province in the south-west of Afghanistan, has more decorative features-stalactite support to balconies, and the circular plan with alternating semi-circular and angular flanges. The Siah Posh minar stands truncated, perhaps abandoned only after the first storey was completed. Ornamentation in stucco on horizontal brick pattern made it a model to inspire the design of the Qutb.

The Qutb Minar forms a part of the Quwwat-ul-Islam mosque complex. It was conceived as a triumphal column proclaiming the might of Islam to the world. The tower was originally called the mazana or the place from where the muezzin gave the call to prayer. It came to be called Qutb Minar much later. May be, because its construction was started by Qutbuddin Aibak or, because it honoured Qutbuddin Bakhtiyar Kaki, the patron sufi saint of Iltutmish, who lived close to the mosque and the tower. Even Firoz Shah Tughlaq refers to the Qutb as "the Minara of Sultan Muizuddin Sam". As a tower from where the muezzin could call the faithful people to prayer, the Qutb was too high to have served this purpose. Besides functioning as a tower which celebrated the advent of new political and religious power in northern India, the Qutb has remained the most stupendous architectural masterpiece of the Sultanate.

Besides the great congregational mosque and the Qutb Minar, Qutbuddin Aibak also began work on Arhai-din-ka-Jhopra, the mosque in Ajmer. Here as in Delhi, the basic mosque structure of corridors and the sanctuary was completed by Aibak in 1200. The stone pillars obtained from the demolished Rajput edifices and a Jain monastery were superimposed one upon another to form the imposing colonnades.

It was left to Iltutmish to add the screen of arches in front of the sanctuary, as it was done by Aibak at the mosque in Delhi. The screen contains seven pointed arches. The central arch is the tallest. It is flanked by three smaller arches on either side. Two smaller arches on each side are cusped or multi-foil, of a distinct Arabian inspiration, making their first appearance on an Islamic building in India. The screen has no triforium or upper storey but has two fluted minarets on the parapet, on both corners of the central arch. An inscription on one of the small minarets mentions Iltutmish: "Sultan-us-Sulatin-us-Shark Abu-ul Muzaffar Ailtamish-us-Sultane Naser Amir-ul Muminin…"

The facade of the arches is covered with rigid geometrical patterns, avoiding the Indian vegetational motifs. The inclusion of a small rectangular panel on the spandrel of each arch is a new feature of the ornament. The Arhai-din-ka-Jhopra, as this mosque is called, has the resoluteness of a well-planned work. The tall stairway in four stages leading upto the elegant portico on the eastern front adds the Imperial look to the structure.

The five domes over the sanctuary are not real domes but the plastered outer surface of corbelled and lantern ceilings. The stone beams laid diagonally across the corners of the square provided an assured support to further additions following the same technique so that only a small opening remained to be filled up by a single slab of stone. The high hills surrounding the Arhai-din-ka-Jhopra, lend it a grandeur befitting agreat congregational mosque of the Sultanate in Ajmer.

Whereas, the mosque and minar were the first structures of their kind to be built in Delhi, the occasion to built a tomb appeared only in 1231 following the death of Nasiruddin Mahmud, the Crown prince of Iltutmish. He was buried at Sultan Garhi, a small fortress-like structure with circular bastions at the corners. The raised octagonal platform was meant to support a small superstructure, which never materialised. On the western wall the mihrab of foliated arch in white marble behind a colonnade of slender pillars, also in marble, provides a charming relief from the grimness of the whole setting. Sultan Garhi, in all likelihood, was a strong outwork of the pre-Sultanate days, converted for the new use as a royal tomb, which could also be used for private ceremonials by the royal family.

It is, however, the small tomb of Iltutmish (1235) which is a real gem of architecture. This small structure of 12.5m side, pierced by tall entrance arches on

facing page. Qutb Minar, Delhi.

above left. Siahposh Minar, Afghanistan right. Jam Minaret, Afghanistan

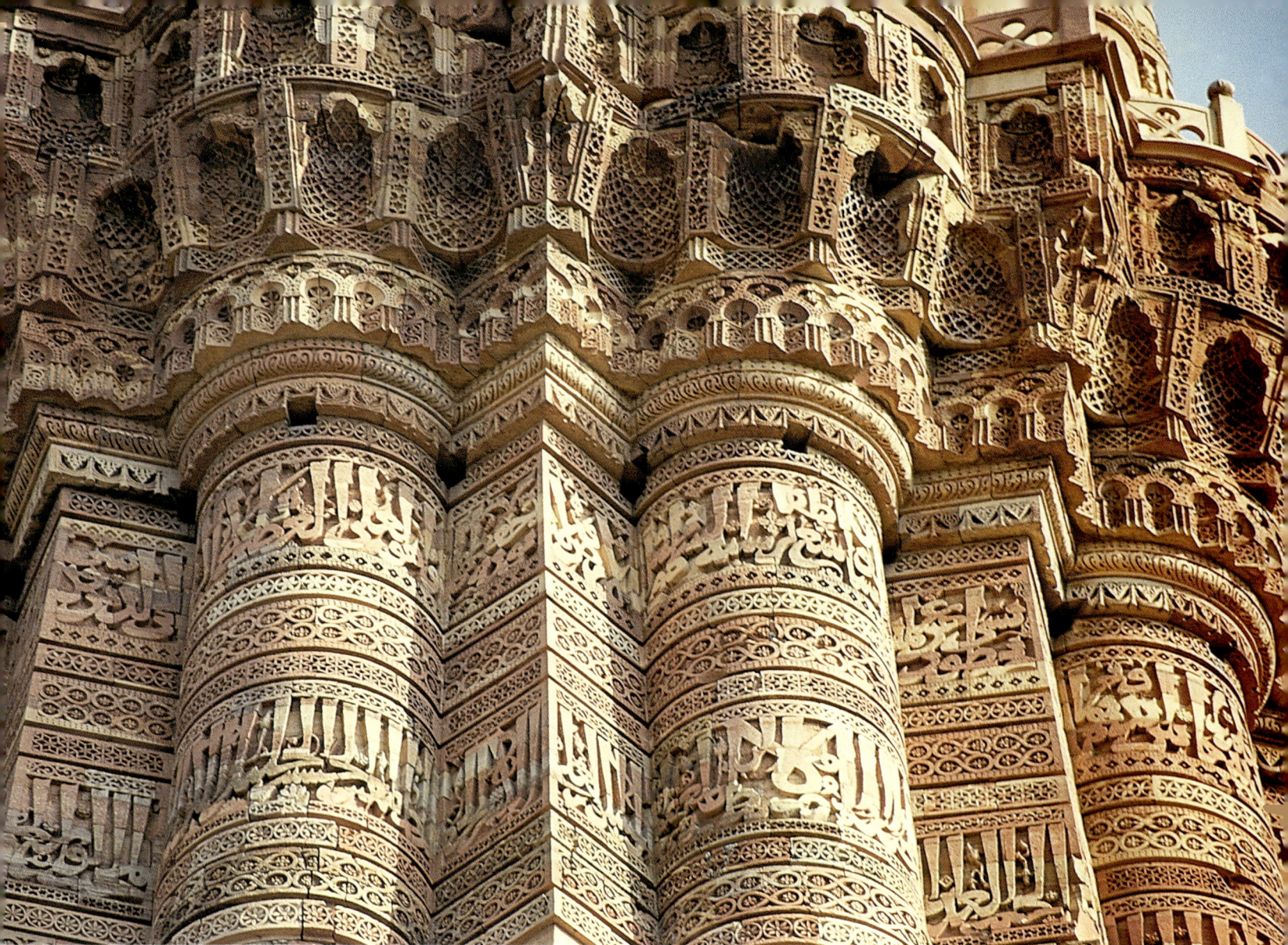

east, north and south sides, stands behind the northern wing of arches on the mosque screen. The exterior has a rather severe look in red sandstone. The interior walls are covered with the most lavish ornamentation with geometrical arabesque and bands of exquisite floral motifs. The inscriptional panels in Kufic, Tughra and Nashtaliq characters evidence perfection of stonecraft. These inscriptions contain nearly thirty chapters of the Quran and themes relating to the eternal Paradise as reward to the faithful servant of God on the Day of Judgement. The mihrab on the western wall has tasteful ornamentation in white marble. The crypt chamber has remained closed to reveal any of its secrets. The tomb is without a dome at present. Here was attempted the first squinch arch dome which, in the absence of the true arch or true vault, either collapsed too soon or was never accomplished. The squinch required projecting a small or similar contrivance across the upper part of the angle of the square hall where it converts the space into an octagon, to be further transformed into a 16 sided form on which the circular rim of the drum could be raised. The cenotaph, in the centre of the hall, is in white marble covered with rich ornamentation. The whole structure, originally designed for the Sultan's tomb, is an outstandig achievement in surface ornamentation.

Water scarcity in the Mehrauli area, the seat of Old Delhi, prompted Iltutmish to excavate a large tank at the southern end of the township. Hauz-i-Shamsi as it is called, was later desilted by Alauddin Khilji and Firoz Shah Tughlaq. He also constructed the Gandak ki Baoli, close to the dargah of his patron saint Bakhtiyar Kaki. The stepped well is in five tiers with a circular well at the southern end reached by a flight of 105 steps. The *baoli* measures 39.9m north-south and 10.4m east-west with galleries of double-storeyed arched rooms on both east and west sides. Masonry construction in coarse rubble stone in uniform size is lined up with horizontal bands of large stone slabs for strength. Iltutmish also had Anangpal II's large tank in the Lal Kot area excavated and enlarged, giving a square shape to the upper terrace. Use of iron clamps and lime mortar for binding the large slabs can still be observed doing their duty well after centuries. Descent to the water has been arranged through three stages. Blocks of stone on the southern and western sides have stone mason's markings for identification of the area where these stones had to be ultimately fixed.

Iltutmish is also credited with the building of a big mosque and a Idgah in Budayun. The mosque has undergone extensive repairs and alteration to provide any information of the original

facing page. First floor of the Qutb Minar.

left. Layout plan of the 'Adhai Din ka Jhopra' mosque, Ajmer

below. 'Adhai Din ka Jhopra' mosque at Ajmer.

plan. The grave of Razia Sultan, daughter of Iltutmish and ruler of Delhi between 1236 and 1240, lies in an inconspicuous corner near Turkman Gate. It is open to the sky.

The 'House of Balban' ruled for merely twenty four years following 1266. The only noteworthy architectural contribution of this brief period is Balban's tomb where the true Islamic arch makes its first appearance in the country. The coarse masonry of rubble covered with plaster is rather rough and unimpressive. The true arch, using radiating voussoirs, indicates the confidence acquired by Indian artisans in essaying Islamic forms and architecture. Besides, the second half of the thirteenth century saw the arrival of many architects and scholars from west Asia following the devastation caused there by the Mongols. There architects might have lent a helping hand to the Indian architects in perfecting the technique of building the true Islamic arch.

The Khiljis, an Afghanised-Turks group, from the village of Khalji near Ghazni in eastern Afghanistan, founded the rule of Khilji dynasty (1290-1320). Allauddin Khilji (1296-1316), the most powerful king, had visions of a world conquest. He aspired to create grandest monuments in the whole Islamic world. He planned to extend the area of Quwwat-ul-Islam Masjid four times of Aibak's original work. The work did not progress beyond extension of the screen of arches to the northern side.

The rubble core stumps of the arches did not rise over 2-3m. Of the three magnficent gateways planned, only one at the south-east corner could be completed and work on the minar also had to be abandoned at the first stage itself.

The Alai Darwaza (1305), part of Alauddin's mosque extension programmes, is the most magnificent gateway and the pride of the Islamic architecture in India. It is known for its horse-shoe or pointed arch entrances with spear-head decoration on the intrados. The perforated screen windows are framed within rectangular bands of elegantly calligraphed borders of eulogical Persian instead of Quranic verses in white marble and red sandstone. The Saljuk Turks seeking shelter in Aladdin's capital, influenced work at the Alai Darwaza.

The interior of the square hall (10.9m side) lies under a ceiling raised over squinch arches or semi-vaults of pointed arches recessing these one within the other in the 'phase of transition'. The carving of floral arabesques on the inner sides of the arches has a definite stencilled surface remarkable for its effect on stone. The semi-circular arch opening towards the inner mosque court has a shallow trefoil outline not particularly Islamic in concept.

The exterior of the Alai Darwaza is noteworthy for its double-storeyed facade. On both sides of the splendid archways, except on the north where it merges with the colonnades of the mosque extension, an additional false storey divides the whole height into two horizontal zones. Each side thus has a set of two oblong panels in the upper storey and a couple of arches with receding

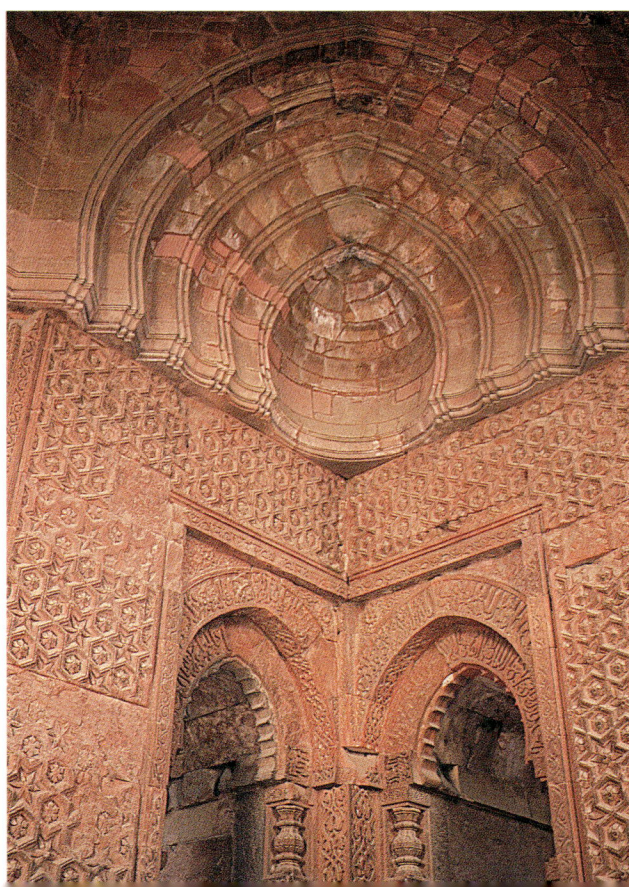

facing page, top. Alai Darwaza at the Qutb, Delhi.

facing page, bottom left. Interior of 'Adhai Din ka Jhopra' mosque, Ajmer.

facing page, bottom right. Interior of Alai Darwaza, Delhi.

right. Detail of the polychromatic decoration on the Alai Darwaza.

the other closed with an ornamental jali screen. The rectangular panel enclosing the central arch rises a little above the parapet behind which rises the modest semi-circular dome crowned with an amalak finial. The effect of the whole architectural composition is extremely pleasing. In fact, the confidence with which its different architectural components are coordinated reveals the experience and maturity of the builder and craftsman. Even as the only completed part of a huge building project, the Alai Darwaza is the most artistic and perfectly finished architectural achievement of the early Islamic rule in India.

The work on Alauddin's minar, intended to dwarf the Qutb in height, had to be abandoned in 1316 following his death. Only the rubble core of the first stage of the minar was ready. Its thirty two angular flutings and shallow curved recesses indicate the design of the exterior. Inside, the core pillar stands with a ramp winding its way up toward the top. In its unfinished condition, the Alai Minar symbolises the unrealised ambition of Alauddin Khilji who lies buried in a domeless structure, unfinished and severely damaged. On either side of the large square cenotaph chamber are two narrow compartments separated by passages. A few rooms, on the tomb's western side, formed the madarsa, the first of its kind in Delhi.

The Jamat Khana mosque at the Nizamuddin dargah closely follows the architectural features of the Alai Darwaza. The three wide-arched entrances, lavishly ornamented inscriptional panels, spear-head fringe on the arch intrados and the squinch-arched domes evidence no real desire to experiment with form of structure. The Chisti saint Nizamuddin (1236-1325) refused burial in the cental chamber to which later on Mubarak Khilji (1316-1320) added additional side wings to be converted into a mosque.

Alauddin Khilji also constructed a water reservoir-Hauz-i-Alai, better known as Hauz Khas. This was a public utility project collecting rainwater in an immense stretch of land. The acute shortge of water in this rocky terrain, first seat of the Sultanate, compelled rulers to devise schemes for harnessing dwindling water resources, inadequate for the growing population. Alauddin Khilji also constructed a bridge of ten massive arches over the Gambhiri river below the ramparts of the Chittaur fort. The bridge, built in 1303 is still in use though the gateways and towers at both ends have since been destroyed.

The last example of Khilji architecture can be seen at Bayama, in Rajasthan. This is the Ukha Masjid, built by Sultan Qutbuddin Mubarak, the last Khilji ruler (1316-1320). Except for the spear-head fringe and the 'keel' arches, the mosque has little to

distinguish itself.

The importance of Qila Rai Pithora or 'old Delhi' declined towards the end of the thirteenth century prompted by two factors: the increasing water scarcity in the capital and each new ruler identifying his political worth with the building of a new city. Unconsciously, the city started shifting toward the river providing more freedom of space, movement, and of course, greenery. Balban's grandson Kaikubad founded a new pleasure city-Kilokhiri on the river front, near the site of Indraprastha, in 1287. Later,

Jalaluddin Khilji (1290-1296) added a few new structures to this township, a sahr nau (new city). Ghiyaspur, the present locality of Nizamuddin, was already a flourishing suburb, peopled by the saint's disciples an refugees from Khurasan and central Asia.

Compelled by frequent and fierce forays by Mongols, Alauddin Khilji decided, in 1303, to build a strong fortified city-called Siri. It was located between Kilokhiri and the old Delhi. The plain of Siri was used as Lashkar (army encampment) by Alauddin and elevated as Darul Khilafa after 1303. Siri had huge battlemented circular

bastions on its massive walls providing in-built passage for the secret movement of troops. Delhi's vulnerability to invasions was highlighted during Taraghai's invasion in 1303 forcing Alauddin Khilji to abandon his prolonged campaigning and taking fortresses (lashkar kashiwa hisar giri). He built a grand hazar sutun palace outside the circular walls of Siri, identified as the Badi Manzil. Sometimes, this palace complex is attributed to Muhammad Tughlaq who also stayed here. However, the proximity of Badi Manzil to the Siri walls suggests that it was a creation of Alauddin Khilji. The splendour of the hazar sutun palace fascinated Timur and ladies in his entourage who made it a point to visit the palace and went back perfectly charmed by its beauty. This palace has been completely destroyed, only the sockets meant to hold the wooden pillars can still be seen carved into the paved courtyard on the top of the high mound.

below. The unfinished Alai Minar at the Qutb.

2

THE TUGHLAQS

In 1320, Ghazi Malik also known as Tughlaq Shah, originally a Turkish slave of Balban, killed Khusraw Shah, the last Khilji sultan, and installed himself on the throne of Delhi as Sultan Ghiyasuddin Tughlaq. He had successfully repulsed four Mongol invasions and was dreaded for his military campaigns. Soon after ascending the throne, Ghiyasuddin started building a magnificent fort on a rocky prominence, south-east of the Qutb Minar or the old Delhi at a site he had chosen when only a soldier of the Khiljis. It was a defence-cum-residential citadel with mammoth ramparts and frowning double-storeyed battlemented towers and bastions. It had no palaces of luxury but merely a residence of Ghiyasuddin, a warrior king determined to extend the territories under his control. Tughlaqabad, the new fort, was the first of those great complexes which included a city, a fort and a palace to meet the new residential and military requirements of the ruler, a much more improved version of Alauddin Khilji's fortress city-Siri.

The Tughlaqabad fort had nearly 52 gateways on its 6.5km circumference. Within the strong walls were palaces, mosques, audience halls, markets, subterranean chambers and dark and winding corridors. The battered fortifications of Tughlaqabad, built in the fashion of Arabian camp cities which had sloping brick walls, were to become characteristic of the Tughlaq architecture. The mammoth fort, with its impregnable defences was hardly completed within the four years of Ghiyasuddin's rule when it was abandoned and lay deserted, open to the elements following his death in 1324. The ponderous megalithic stones on the ramparts crumbled and the fort soon turned into a wilderness of ruins and decaying structures.

The reason why Tughlaqabad was abandoned lies in the desire of each new ruler to build his own fort and city: the desire which urged Muhammad Tughlaq (1325-1351) to build a new fort-Adilabad, close to Tughlaqabad. Popular belief, however ascribes Tughlaqabad's pathetic ruinous state to the curse of the renowned Sufi saint Nizamuddin Auliya, who was a contemporary of Ghiyasuddin and who lived through the reigns of seven sultans of Delhi.

An interesting episode highlighting conflict between the sultan and the saint, took place when Ghiyasuddin forbade his men to work on the baoli, built by the saint at Ghiyaspur where he lived, because it interfered with work at the Tughlaqabad fort. The saint miraculously caused water to emit light so that men could now work at night. This greatly irked Ghiyasuddin who, then out on a campaign, swore to settle matters with the saint once he returned to Delhi. The saint quipped "Hunuz Dilli dur ast" (Delhi is yet far away). As things took shape, when the sultan reached Delhi, his son arranged for him a grand

previous pages. Tughlaqabad Fort.

right. Sketch depicting fortress opposite Tughlaqabad fort housing the tomb of Ghiyassuddin Tughlaq.

facing page. Tomb of Ghiyassuddin Tughlaq.

reception. Accidentally the caparisoned elephants lined up to salute the sultan, started running away, causing commotion and bringing down the wooden canopy crashing on the Sultan's head, causing instantaneous death. Sure, the sultan never reached Delhi alive and the fort was abandoned and left unpeopled in fulfilment of the saint's prophesy: "ya rahe usar, ya base gujar" (either stay barren or be peopled by the Gujjar tribe). Historians debate over the authenticity of this episode and saint Nizamuddin's complicity in the murder of Ghiyasuddin Tughlaq by his son Ulugh Khan, who ascended the throne as Muhammad Tughlaq.

The *baoli* at the dargah of Nizamudin, one of the most sacred spots in Delhi, was built to provide relief to people who thronged in ever-increasing numbers at the saint's doorstep. It is rectangular in plan and enclosed by strong walls of dressed stone. Steps leading to the water are on the northern side where a huge gateway provides entrance to the shrine complex. The tank, 55m long and 38m wide, has many structures on the western side. An arcaded passage from the north end winds its way to the Jamat Khana Masjid. In the precincts of the Khilji mosque, lies the dargah of Nizamuddin, the most respected saint of the Chishtiya order in the country.

The tomb of Sultan Ghiyasuddin Tughlaq stands within an independent, self-contained outwork. It is pentagonal in plan with conical bastions at the angles. The fortress tomb stands within a huge artificial lake, connected by a 80m long elevated causeway to the awesome fort. The gateway at the tomb has been ingeniously fashioned into a deathtrap for intruders, further strengthened by unexpected traverses. The inner walls have arched corridors and strong vaulted chambers where the sultan kept his treasures and molten gold for safe keeping. The courtyard has an irregular outline with octagonal pavilions at the angles. The tomb stands in a section with the widest disposition.

The tomb has distinctive look-built in red sandstone with battered walls carrying only discreet and minimum ornamentation with panels in white marble. Of particular interest is the spear-head fringe over the entrance arches raised on columns and beam, an unusual structural element. The arch

and beam shows a convenient fusion of the Islamic arcuate with the indigenous trabeate style of construction. The Indian genius rendered the use of the beam more attractive and acceptable by introducing a bracket under the beam a design favoured by subsequent builders over the centuries to follow. The stark unadorned design is also remarkable for the complete lack of epigraphs. The exhuberance of surface ornamentation as seen on the tomb of Iltutmish and the splendid polychromatic decoration at the Alai Darwaza is conspicuous by its absence at the tomb of Ghiyasuddin Tughlaq. This puritanic streak in decoration was to become a lasting feature of the Tughlaq architecture.

The single, pointed dome at Ghiyasuddin's tomb is crowned with a vase and melon (kalash and amala) motif. The total height of the structure, between the base and the crest, is nearly 25m. The whole structure is considerably influenced by the contemporary brick-built tombs in Multan, particularly the tomb of Rukn-i-Alam, built by Ghiyasuddin himself. The sloping walls and massive strength of the towers and the tomb create an impression of unadorned splendour grim fortifications and an austere interior fit for a soldier "in singular contrast with the elegant and luxuriant garden-tombs of the more settled and peaceful dynasties that succeeded", observes James Fergusson. In view of its highly emphasized battered appearance, Ghiyasuddin Tughlaq's tomb "would be as appropriate more so, indeed if found in the valley of the Nile than on the banks of the Jamna". For its unique conception Ghiyasudin's tomb remains one of the most perfect and beautiful specimens of the Islamic architecture in India.

Muhammad Tughlaq succeeded Ghiyasuddin Tughlaq in 1325, abandoned the Tughlaqabad fort and ordered construction of Adilabad, a new fort adjacent to his father's magnificent, just-completed fort, but perhaps not intended to replace 'old Delhi' as either a commercial or administrative centre. Built like Tughlaqabad, Adilabad had gigantic bastions, towering ramparts and a hazar sutun (thousand pillar hall). Almost every single structure at Adilabad has been destroyed leaving it a mere heap of stones. Some portions of gateways is all that has survived at Adilabad. Another small fortress Nai ka Kot, also built near the Tughlaqabad fort, has also suffered heavy destruction.

Muhammad Tughlaq built Jahanpanah, a new city by enclosing within a long meandering wall the populated areas between Siri and Qila Rai Pithora. The city had thirteen gates, as mentioned by Timur-seven on the south side bearing towards the east, and six on the north side bearing towards the west. It was in the vicinity of Siri that Muhammad Tughlaq supposedly built a hazar sutun, perhaps the Dar-Sara as described by Ibn Battuta. The only surviving portion of this famous palace is Badi Manzil, now called Bijay Mandal. Bases of wooden pillars have been excavated on the terrace to show existence of a large audience hall. The octagonal tower from where the sultan observed his soldiers parading and other royal ceremonies is in sheer ruins.

Satpulah, a dam constructed in 1326 by Muhammad Tughlaq, has survived in full preservation. There are eleven spans of which the main seven spans controlled the flow of water into the artificial lake. Two octagonal towers at both ends of the bridge contain rooms for guards and a school. This dam, a double-storeyed construction with narrow stairs at both leading to the top, is a remarkable example of medieval engineering. It is still in use after nearly six hundred years.

The number of monuments belonging to the 26 year long reign of Muhammad Tughlaq is rather too small. He was one of the most enlightened, though capricious, monarch of his age, the first to think of an all-India administration. His move to shift capital to Devagiri, renamed Daulatabad, as the second administrative centre of his kingdom, ended in a complete disaster, bringing in only misery to the people. There were uncontrollable rebellions throughout his kingdom which became unwieldy and soon started disintegrating into pieces. Famines and plague caused great misery to the people. Nothing worked for Muhammad Tughlaq and toward his end he was engulfed in a sea of hatred. His death in 1551 brought some cheer to the people.

In order to save the mortal remains of Muhammad Tughlaq from the hostile people, Firoz Shah, his successor, had buried him in a modest grave within the Dar'ul-Aman, the octagonal pavilion situated to the north-east of Ghiyasuddin Tughlaq's tomb. Firoz Shah obtained letters of forgiveness by paying monetary compensation to those who had been mutilated by him (Muhammad Tughlaq) and from the heirs of those whom he had killed, duly attested by witnesses. Firoz sealed them in a box at the head of the deceased Sultan's grave. "It was a subtle comment on the deceased Sultan's policies and nothing more insinuating could have been done to malign him", observes historian K.A Nizami. There is no tombstone over the grave except a rubble and plaster covering and in the words of the Bard of Stratford-upon-Avon: "When that this body did contain a spirit, A kingdom for it was too small a bound; But now two paces of the vilest earth is room enough…"

Firoz Shah Tughlaq (1351-88), third renowned ruler of the Tughlaq dynasty, inherited a treasury with much depleted and shrinking finances caused by his predecessor's political extravagances. The capital was in a state of perceptible decline. Water shortage was acute. Maintenance of the four existing cities-Old Delhi, Siri, Tughlaqabad and Jahanpanah was virtually beyond his means. Firoz Shah chose to move his capital to an economically more viable position along the river Yamuna from the ones set on the rocky grounds. Kotla, north of Indraprastha, embraced eighteen villages stretching upto Kushk-i-Shikar and the second Ashokan Pillar at the base of the northern Ridge. As historian M. Athar Ali observes, the founding of Kotla "set the seal on the decline of the Delhi of the Sultanate with its sites upon and around the rocky wastes and shifted it compellingly to the lower lands to the north and north-east".

Firoz Shah Tughlaq was the first known conservationist amongst rulers of the Delhi Sultanate. "One of God's favours to me", Firoz mentions in his Fatuhat, "has been the fact that I have been able to repair and renew the buildings of past kings and great amirs, and I have given this repair work precedence over my own constructions". He did much restoration work at the Jami Masjid of old Delhi, the Minar of Delhi, the Shamsi Tank, the Alai Tank, the Madarsa of Iltutmish and the completion of the Jahanpanah walls. Firoz Shah remained a prolific builder, credited with some 50 canals, 40 mosques, 30 colleges, 100 palaces, 200 public inns, 150 bridges, 1200 gardens and 30 towns, many in places far off from the capital.

The citadel of Kotla had three splendid palaces, a large and grand mosque, reception halls, galleries, gardens, a baoli and a unique pyramidal structure to uphold the Ashokan Pillar he had brought from Ambala. Most of these buildings are rubble work covered with heavy plaster without any surface decoration. The masonry lacked the strength and finish of the architecture of the preceding Khilji period. The immigration of skilled stone masons and artisans to Daulatabad perhaps accounts for the unimpressive look of the many structures of the Tughlaq period. Still from the ruins of Kotla one can easily identify some better-known structures.

The Jami Masjid at Kotla has survived in its open spectacular courtyard and a portion of the Western Wall. Raised on a terrace of vaulted chambers, the mosque could accommodate nearly ten thousand men at prayer. According to Franklin who visited the mosque in 1793, it had four cloisters, the domed roofs of which were supported by 260 stone columns, each about 5m high. The centre of the courtyard lay under an 8m high brick and stone octagonal dome. On the central column Firoz Shah is believed to have inscribed his great achievements, the place now indicated only by the pit at the centre.

Close to the Jami Masjid stands a pyramidal structure, a triple-storeyed construction of vaulted cells around a solid core with stairs at the corners leading to the uppermost terrace where Firoz Tughlaq planted the Ashokan Pillar he had transported from Ambala. It is a remarkable structure in northern India. The other Ashokan Pillar, also brought by Firoz Tughlaq, was planted

facing page. Ruins of a pillared hall at Firoz Shah Kotla.

right. Baoli at Firoz Shah Kotla.

bottom. Tomb of Firoz Shah Tughlaq at Hauz Khas, Delhi.

at Kushk-i-Shikar. To the east of this pyramidal structure can be seen the ruins of a grand reception hall, identifiable for its square plan marked by bases of huge stone columns.

The three-tiered structure of a small and functional baoli is nearly intact. The water supply runs through transverse pipelines and cistern provisions, harnessing to advantage its proximity to the river which then flowed below the ramparts. During the summer months the baoli functioned as a cool retreat for the royal inmates of the palace.

Some ruins of Firozian structures can be seen at the northern ridge. This cluster has a mosque, a *baoli* and a hunting lodge called Kushk-i-Shikar or Peerghaib. The secret underground passage connecting this place with Kotla collapsed at various places and have been sealed.

The tomb of Firoz Shah Tughlaq stands in Huaz Khas. It has a severely plain exterior with battered walls built in rubble masonry and covered with lime plaster. The entrance doorway uses a lintel and brackets. The cupola shaped dome rises over squinches. The most interesting feature of the tomb is the Sanchi-style railing protecting the entrance. The Madarsa consists of oblong pillared halls, each three aisles deep and square domed chambers. The residential portion formed the lower storey with

oriel windows opening toward the vast reservoir built by Alauddin Khilji. The north-eastern enclosure contains five chattris, housing the graves of renowned teachers. This Madarsa building is perhaps the largest structure meant for this purpose.

The architecture of mosques remains the most outstanding contribution of Firoz Shah Tughlaq. Austere in style, high plinthed and fortress like in their battered walls and corner bastions these Firozian mosques are symbols of royal power. Massive gateways atop a high flight of steps lead into these grand congregational mosques, built by Khan-i-Jahan Maqbul Khan Tilangani and his son Khan-i-Jahan Junah Khan in the 1370. The chief mosques of this period are: Kali Masjid at Turkman Gate, Kali Masjid at Nizamuddin, Khirki Masjid at Sheikh Serai, Beghampuri Masjid near Malviya Nagar and Shah Alam Masjid near Wazirabad.

The Beghampuri Masjid (1370) is the largest mosque with a stately courtyard. The tall arched pylon with tapering turrets attached to its quoins on the western wall is the most distinctive architectural feature of this mosque. The three bay deep corridor surrounding the courtyard adds depth to the structure. It is sometimes believed to be the Jami Masjid built by Muhammad Tughlaq, near the hazar sutun at Jahanpanah. The tall pylon

obliterating the view of the dome over the sanctuary did not find favour with the builders and patrons of architecture in Delhi. In Jaunpur, another Firozian stronghold, this pylon was to be used in a much more dignified and enlarged form at the Sharqi mosques.

The Khirki Masjid (1375) occupying an area of 87 sq m is built on a platform over vaulted basement chambers. The massive gateway at the entrance is flanked by two strong tapering turrets and projects about 7m from the main structural wall of the mosque. The Khirki Masjid is a covered mosque, a bold architectural experiment. The ceiling is supported on 180 columns and 60 pilasters. The interior has been designed on a cruciform plan with two rows of east-west and north-south arcades intersecting each other in the centre at right angles, a fine example of the cross-axial variety. The 85 small domes crowning the roof add a new dimension to mosque architecture of the Sultanate. The composition of open spaces alternating with clusters of domes and flat ceiling areas looks very impressive. The masonry is rather unrefined and lacks strength and stability required for such massive structures. The Khirki Masjid is one of the most beautiful mosques in Delhi.

The Kali Masjid at Nizamuddin (1370) repeats most of the

structural features of the Khirki Masjid without achieving the latter's magnificence. The Kali Masjid at Turkman Gate is another massive mosque built in the architectural style and pattern of the mosque at Nizamuddin. Much in use and regularly whitewashed, the interior of these two mosques still retains its original character. The small, contemporary Shah Alam mosque at Wazirabad, built for a saint, has a five arched facade. The simple prayer hall has two bays and five aisles surmounted by three domes. A chilla or royal balcony is approached from outside for the exclusive use of women. This mosque shows a predilection for openness, a feature used to greater advantage by the Lodis and Mughals.

An important point to note about these mosques is the complete absence of any Quranic inscriptions and calligraphy for surface decoration. Khan-i-Jahan Tilangani, builder of these mosques in Delhi, made yet another contribution to architecture in the Imperial capital by building for himself an octagonal tomb (1388-89) recalling in design the seventh century mosque of Omar at Jerusalem. The central cenotaph chamber is surrounded by a verandah, with three four-centred arches on each of the eight sides, standing under a prominently projecting cave (chajja). On the roof eight cupolas rise above the embrasures of the parapet encircling the dome. Built in the open, behind the dargah of Nizamuddin, this bold experiment in tomb architecture was chosen as the architectural form for the royal tombs by the Sayyid and Lodi rulers.

Firoz Shah also had a dam built at the north-west corner of the Shah Alam mosque. It is a nine-arched construction over a fast flowing branch of the Yamuna. It measures about 47m in length and 5m in width and contains a sluice chamber. This structure is still in use by residents of the villages across the stream.

The only other structure of the Tughlaq period in Delhi is the small tomb of Sheikh Kabiruddin Auliya (1397) near Malviya Nagar. Closely imitating the tomb of Ghiyasuddin Tughlaq, founder of the dynasty, this tomb has poor construction and little ornamentation. The conical dome covered with plaster was perhaps denuded of its marble casing during Timur's sack of Delhi in 1398. The structure itself indicates a marked decline in the architectural standards achieved earlier.

Among the new cities founded by Firoz Shah Tughlaq are Firozabad (Kotla), Harni Khera, Tughlaqpur Sapdam and Tughlaqpur Kasna. He also constructed and strengthened many a fort throughout his kingdom, most important of these great structures are at Jaunpur and Hissar. The Hissar-i-Firusa has a Darbar Hall, baradari, underground chambers, mosque and a stone column inscribed with details of his achievements. The Jaunpur fort now has only a mosque and Turkish baths as relics of the Firozian era.

Timur's sack of Delhi had irreparably destroyed the prestige of the Sultanate. "In any meaningful sense of the word", as Prof. Gavin R.G. Hambly observes, "the Delhi Sultanate was no more".

facing page. Interior of the Khirki Masjid, Delhi.

below. Beghampuri Masjid, Delhi.

The Lodi tombs. Bada Gumbad and Shish Gumbad and the Bada Gumbad mosque at the lodi gardens, Delhi

Octagonal tomb of Muhammad Shah, Delhi

The wave of destruction which swept over Delhi in the wake of Timur's invasion in 1398 left but little for the Sayyids who came into power in 1414. Khijr Khan (1414-1421) founded the short-lived Sayyid rule of thirty years. The Sayyids declared themselves dependants of Shah Rukh, Timur's successor. No ambitious architectural projects could be imagined from rulers who inherited empty state coffers, ruins of forts and palaces, and an all-round poverty. Surprisingly, the Sayyids left behind a large number of tombs as memorials of their brief, lacklustre rule.

The octagonal style of tomb architecture, initiated in Delhi by Khan-i-Jahan Tilangani at his own tomb (1388) was chosen as model for the new royal tombs. Khijr Khan built his tomb in Khijrabad, a city he founded near Okhla, now completely disappeared. Mubarak Sayyid, the second Sayyid ruler, built Mubarakabad, yet another new city near Khijrabad which was also soon destroyed. The tomb of Mubarak Sayyid (1434) stands in a thickly populated locality in Kotla Mubarakpur. The main entrance to this octagonal tomb is from the southern side. The cenotaph chamber is surrounded by a verandah which has three arched openings on each side of the octagon. The corners, strengthened by buttresses, give it a look of massive structure, further accentuated by a broad low dome crowned by a lantern. There are eight chattris on the roof. The soffit of the ceiling is ornamented with incised and coloured bands of plaster and inscriptions from the Quran.

The tomb of Mubarak Shah (1421-1433) has wide proportions on the ground. The dome over the parapets, surrounded by the chattris, looks a trifle too stunted which gives the elevation an ungainly and ponderous appearance.

The tomb of Muhammad Shah (1434-1443) follows the outline of his predecessor's tomb. The basic design is the same, the tomb chamber surrounded by an octagonal verandah, triple arched-openings on all the eight sides standing under a prominently projecting eave, massive piers and buttressed support at angles of the octagon. The eight elegant chattris at angles of the octagon around the lotus-topped high dome are part of a well-proportioned elevation and do not detract from the impression of good height so essential for an aesthetically satisfying composition. A few flaws observed at the earlier tomb have been remedied, the dome and kiosks have been raised a few feet to achieve an increase in height. The soffit of the dome has some decoration in vibrant colours. All the lines on its elevation are perpendicular excepting those on the angles which are sloped. Both these octagonal tombs are noteworthy for the generous use of stone on the plinths, pillars, piers, pilasters, eaves and kiosks. The tombs of Mubarak Shah and Muhammad Shah have identical proportions.

The tomb of Sikandar Lodi (1489-1517) stands in the Lodi Gardens, earlier called the village of Khairpur. This octagonal tomb follows the architectural style of Muhammad Shah's tomb but has distinguished itself by incorporating a few improvements in the concept of the tomb itself. It marks the first attempt to break away from the gloomy and fortress-like Tughlaq tombs by placing the structure in a garden setting. The ornamental gateway and octagonal turrets at each end of the high-plinthed walled enclosure give it the air of importance suited to the status of the occupant. The dome is also unique. It has two shells of masonry with space in between; an experiment made to increase the height of the outer dome while retaining the ceiling at a height appropriate to the dimensions of the cenotaph chamber. This 'double dome' is the first of its kind in the country though it was already in use in Persia, Iraq and western Asia. The dome is not surrounded by chattris above the parapet which tended to obliterate the view of the dome at the earlier octagonal tombs. The high-walled enclosure of Sikandar Lodi's tomb stands over a stream, once fed by the Yamuna river, recreating the image of paradise so much emphasized in the Char-Bagh gardens around the Mughal tombs.

Square tomb, the other architectural experiment made by the Lodis who succeeded the Sayyids in 1444, was made mostly for tombs of the nobles and ministers. Delhi alone contains a great number of such square tombs, earlier used for the royalty. The Lodis, a tribe from Afghanistan, shared a special relationship with members of other Afghan tribes who supported them. "These tribal chiefs", observes Catherine Asher, "viewed a king not as an absolute but rather as a comrade who was first among equals. In this same manner, these nobles felt that they, too, should merit tombs, formerly a royal perquisite". The large number of square tombs thus accommodates the comrades of the ruler-nobles, chiefs, dignitaries etc. In the absence of inscriptional tablets, the identity of the entombed personage remains open to speculation. Built generally as isolated structures, the square tombs are single-compartment structures without the surrounding verandah or enclosure. If the octagonal tombs are one-third wider than the square tombs, the latter are one-third taller with high domes crowning the cubical structures. The exterior facade is divided in two and sometimes three ornamental arcaded zones with recessed arches sunk in rectangular panels. The central arch is set within a high rectangular panel rising to the height of the structure below the dome. The dome rests on squinches. The walls are straight with accented vertical lines. These square tombs are apparently inspired by the Alai Darwaza minus its exquisite ornament or superior elegance. Mostly local stone has been used on these square tombs giving them a monotonous unvariegated look. These tombs are identified with the respectful appellations given by people i.e. Bade Khan ka Gumbad, Chote Khan ka Gumbad, Dadi-Poti ka Gumbad etc.

Chote Khan ka Gumbad at Kotla Mubarakpur is an important square tomb (1490) though it provides no relevant information about the identity of the owner. All inscriptions are from the Quran. The structure is elegant. Its double-storeyed facade contains the central arch framed within an iwan. On both sides of the iwan and on both tiers is a set of two recessed arches, eight in all. The lintel-and-bracket with stone pilasters are provided in the iwan in the middle of each face on the east, north and south. The western side is closed to accommodate the mihrab. The parapet is decorated with merlons and pinnacles rising over each corner of the iwan which rises slightly over the parapet. Four corner pillared kiosks (chattris) add some splendour to the superstructure dominated by a high dome. In fact, the Chote Khan ka Gumbad is an excellent example of the best features of the square tomb. There is no attempt to include minarets to the structure which has been modeled after the Alai Darwaza.

As an architectural style, the square tomb found general acceptance. In absence of any determined effort to break away from the practice of assigning square tombs to the nobles and dignitaries, the square tomb emerged as the trend and the norm which remained long in use, uninterrupted by changes in the ruling dynasties. The other examples of the square tomb show that the royalty did not interfere in the building of these tombs anywhere in the city.

The Bada Gumbad (1490) dominates the Lodi Garden with its high spherical dome raised on a twelve-sided drum with no chattris around it. Sometimes believed to be the entrance to the mosque behind it, the Bada Gumbad appears to be an independent creation, the tomb of some unidentified personage. The iwans or the rectangular frames contain the arched entrances with the lintel-and-bracket entrances. The brackets, in red sandstone, heavy and elegantly fashioned, provide the only note of contrast and ornament on this sombre but massive structure. The tombstone is missing which misleads one to believe the Bada Gumbad to be gateway to the mosque. All the four sides are open and there is no mihrab. Inscriptions carved over entrances are from the Quran. Most of the pinnacles rising over the parapet have crumbled but Bad Gumbad by its sheer magnificent proportions, remains the most splendid tomb of its kind.

Shish Gumbad (1490) has a double-storeyed exterior with a careful arrangement of horizontal lines crossing the vertical lines. There are traces of some remarkable ornamentation with turquoise, blue glazed tiles on the central frieze on the exterior. The western wall has a mihrab. The three other sides have arched entrances set within a projected frame. The soffit of the dome carries some elegant ornamentation in incised plasterwork, floral patterns with Quranic inscriptions, typical of the age.

Kotla Mubarakpur is the core of the city founded by Mubarak Shah Sayyid in 1433. The square tombs in this locality are the other examples of tombs of this class. Kale Khan Ka Gumbad stands in isolated grandeur, built in 1481, during Bahlol Lodi's reign, this tomb has a ceiling decorated with elegant painted-work in stucco. At the northern end of Kotla Mubarakpur is a small cluster of three tombs. Bade Khan ka Gumbad is the largest structure, built in 1510, this square tomb has a triple-storeyed exterior. The three arcaded zones on each side of the central arch have three arches on each tier. The

massive dome lends the structure an air of importance. The soffit of the dome is decorated with incised and painted-plaster bands. Four elegant chattris stand on the corners above the parapet, an infrequent structural element on these square tombs.

The tomb of Darya Khan Lohani, in Kidwai Nagar, stands on an extensive platform with corner chattris. Darya Khan served all kings of the Lodi dynasty with distinction. Bagh-i-Alam ka Gumbad (1501) is the three-tiered structure over the grave of Miyan Seikh Shihabuddin Taj Khan, a saint. Also in the vicinity of the saint's tomb are the two tombs known as Dadi-Poti tombs. Rama Krishna Puram, Zamrudpur and many other localities of Delhi contain a great number of square tombs.

The most distinctive, though a simple tomb in architectural terms, belongs to Bahlol Lodi. Built in 1488 the modest structure forms part of the dargah of Roshan Chiragh Dilli. It is a 44 feet square hall with 8 feet high triple arched openings on each side. The spandrels of the red sandstone arches carry medallions. A heavy chajja provides protection from rain and sun. The structure is crowned with five inconspicuous domes. This is the first open-hall tomb in Delhi, setting an example for the Chausath Khamba tomb (1623-24).

The Lodis, who introduced the square tomb into the Islamic architecture in India, were also responsible for making another notable contribution-the small single aisle mosque with three or five arched openings. The beauty of these mosques owes much to the profuse use of calligraphy, inlaid coloured stones and a much-emphasized central portal. These mosques generally are built within a walled enclosure but have a pronounced effect of openness.

The Bada Gumbad Masjid (1494) also called the Jami Masjid of Sikandar Lodi, is a small ornate mosque. It has tapering turrets conical bastions at the rear side and oriel windows supported on stone bracket. The five-arched facade is elegant. The height of all the arches is the same but the width varies. The curves of the arches lack resolution. The receding planes of arches and the spandrels are covered with the most lavish ornamentation in stucco. The soffit of the dome, frames of niches and arches are covered with hundreds of Quranic inscriptions. Perhaps there existed a central ablution tank between the mosque and the guesthouse, now filled up and raised as a platform. The structure and decoration of the mosque are strikingly different from the Bada Gumbad tomb, standing close to its southern wing. The latter could not have been the gateway to the mosque.

Moth ki Masjid (1500) is a prominent mosque of the Lodi period. Miyan Bhuwa, a minister of Sikandar Lodi, built this mosque on the proceeds of a seed of grain picked up by the Sultan. The minister multiplied the seed in a field and earned enough to build this mosque. The ornamental gateway to the mosque has been much damaged but the mosque is well preserved. The whole structure stands on a 2m high plinth. The five-arched dignified façade is 38m long. The central arch is enclosed within a highly ornate iwan, with an oriel window above the archway, panels with sunken arched niches on both sides along the elevation. The side piers are slightly battered.

The facade of the mosque makes a judicious combination of red sandstone with grey granite and quartzose for an extremely pleasant and colourful effect. The spandrel of the arches has been decorated with medallions in plaster. The interior, composed of five bays, is elegant. Both squinches and corbelled pendentives have been employed in the 'phase of transition'. In marked contrast to the Bada Gumbad Masjid, the conical bastions attached to the angles of the rear of the structure have been replaced with octagonal double-storeyed towers with arched openings and chajjas supported on brackets on all sides. Oriel windows have been provided to enhance the architectural beauty of the structure. The mosque, built fully in stone, is topped with three domes overlooking the spacious courtyard.

Rajon ki baoli (1516) is one of the major public welfare projects of Sikandar Lodi. Built near Adham Khan's tomb in Mehrauli, the baoli has more than 70 steps descending to the water level. The high stone walls on three sides contain rooms for visitors. The lowest line of rooms lies occasionally submerged in water during rains. A small mosque and an open pavilion with a gorgeously painted ceiling, stand near the baoli. Another baoli attributed to the Lodis is the Ugar Sen ki baoli, near the Connaught Place, scene of water frolics among the local children. It is a purely functional structure.

The mosque and tomb of Sheikh Fazlullah or Jalal Khan Jalali known as Jamali Kamali Masjid, was built in 1528-29 at the onset of the Mughal rule in India. In strict chronolofical order, this mosque belongs to the Mughal period but, since the style is

facing page. Bada Gumbad mosque, Delhi

right. Rajon ki Baoli in Mehrauli, Delhi

pre-eminently Lodi in character, it is included here as culminating the architecture of the Sayyid and Lodi period. Jamali, the poet saint lived during the reigns of Sikandar Lodi, Babur and Humayun and died in 1536 when Agra was the capital.

The Jamali Kamali Masjid is built within an enclosed area. It has a five arched facade. The central pointed arch, flanked by two smaller arched on either side, has a spear-head fringe and is contained within a high rectangular frame with stone turrets at the quoins of the frame. These turrets with alternating rounded and angular flutings and divided by string courses, are in four stages. Within the central arch is set a smaller double-planed arch topped by an oriel window. The side arches on both sides are triple planed. The piers carry ornamental arches sunk into oblong panels. The spandrels are decorated with stone rosettes in high relief. There is a frieze of ornamental arches over the twin arches on both sides of the central arch. The structure is crowned with a single high cylindrical dome topped with an open lotus. The rear wall has two octagonal towers and three oriel windows. There are staircases at both ends leading to the gallery above.

The tomb of the saint is, in fact, a small room which also contains the grave of Kamali whose identity remains unknown. The flat ceiling is covered with incised and painted floral designs of the most elaborate and exquisite quality.

The Jamali Kamali Masjid marks the last stages of an architectural tradition which was destined to continue for a few more decades after the fall of the Lodis in 1526. "partly on account of its prestige and ancient lineage, and partly because the unsettled state of the country under the early Mughals", which "precluded anything else from taking its place". The architectural tradition followed its own course of evolution. The use of fine ashlar masonry in place of rubble and plaster work envisages a new scheme of improving the quality of architecture in general. A better and more elaborately finished workmanship is in evidence at Moth ki Masjid and Jamali Kamali Masjid. Both remain examples of a style striving toward structural maturity with work in red sandstone interspersed with white marble, a connecting link between the architectural style of the Sultanate and the oncoming style of the Mughals.

4

KASHMIR & MULTAN

There are very few remains of the earliest Hindu and Buddhist structures in Kashmir but the few wood structures from the early Muslim rule, beginning from 1339, have survived to this day in a nearly original form. Building in wood has had a long tradition in this mountainous region, governed by the climate and need of the people. Wood was the easiest building material obtainable from dense forests on the high hills. Laying one log horizontally on another usually crosswise in the form of 'headers and stretchers', as in brickwork, was the most convenient method of construction. Even the most ancient wooden bridges, built on the river Jhelum in Srinagar, have served their purpose successfully over the centuries.

The mosque and the tomb, built in wood, generally follow the same architectural principles: a long cubical structure of the interior hall or chamber; a pyramidal roof in tiers upon tiers of wood; and a slender spire at the apex of the structure. A square open pillared pavilion included between the top of the roof and below the spire appears at the mosques.

The Jami Masjid, built 1400 by Sikandar Butshikan and enlarged by his son Zainul Abidin, is the most representative of the timber architecture in Kashmir. It was burnt down thrice, once in the fifteenth century and twice in the seventeenth century and rebuilt on the original lines of construction. The impressive court, 87m side externally, is enclosed within a high brick wall. There are colonnades on all the four sides internally. At the centre of each side is a hall. These four halls are covered with pyramidal roofs, open pavilions and spires. The lofty pillars demarcating the aisles and cloisters measure between 7.5m and 15m in height. These aisles are four bay deep on three sides and three bay deep on the fourth side. The whole interior is a veritable forest of stately columns, totaling 378.

The Shah Hamadan Masjid in Srinagar is an impressive structure. The mosque derives its name from its builder Mir Sayyid Ali Hamadani (1385) an Iranian Sufi saint of the Kubrawiyya order who is believed to have reached Srinagar in 1381 and converted the Brahmin priest of the Kali temple. The mosque stands on the ruins of an ancient temple on the right bank of the Jhelum river. It is a double storeyed structure, square in plan with projecting balconies, pyramidal roof topped by an open pavilion under the spire. The total height of the structure, from the ground level to the apex of the spire, is nearly 40m. Logs used in the lower portion are trimmed square and laid in alternate courses as in brickwork. The arcades, verandahs, porticos and carved panels all contribute to the charm of the structure. The planks over the pyramidal section of the roof are covered with multiple layers of birch bark for waterproofing since

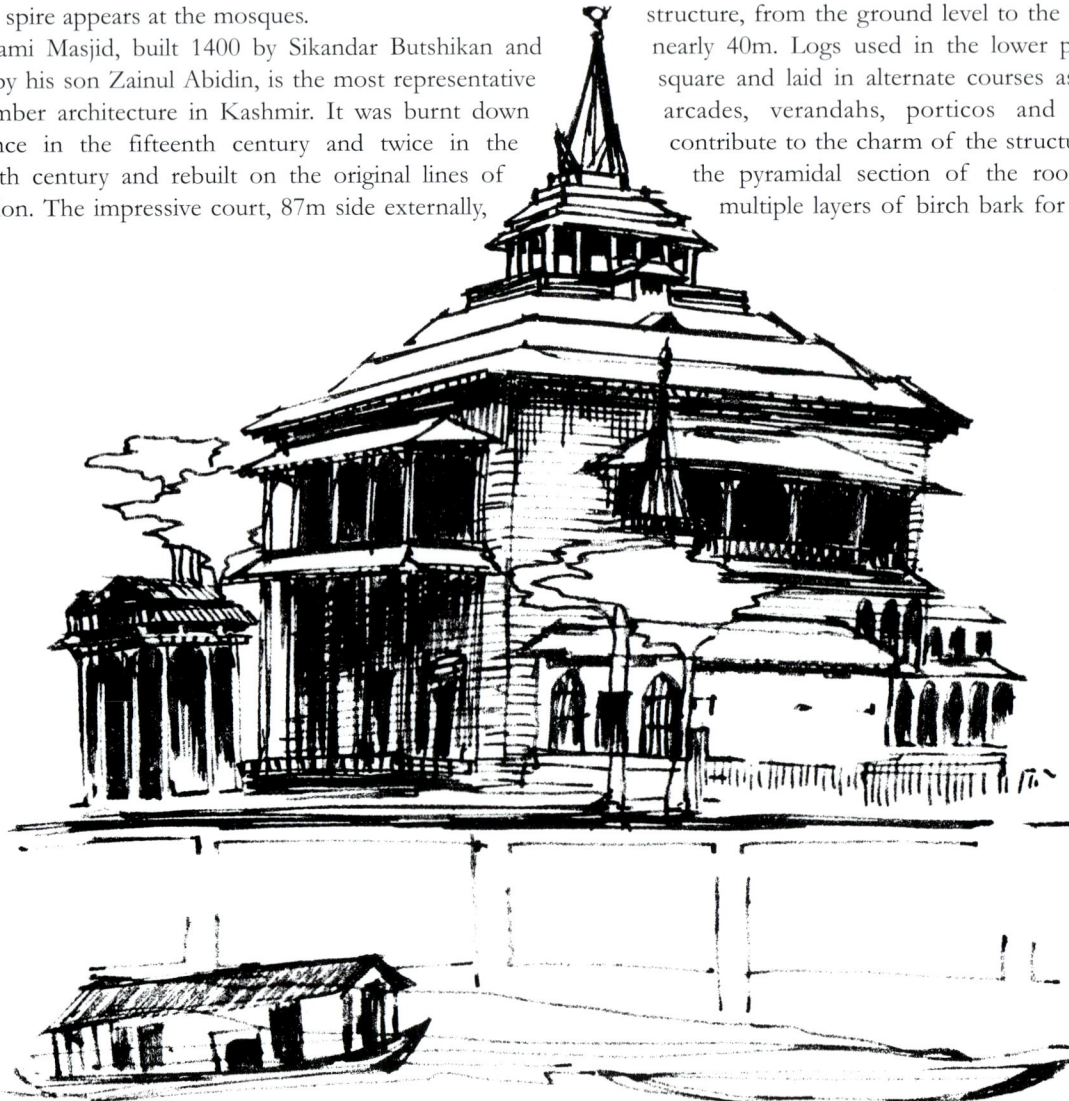

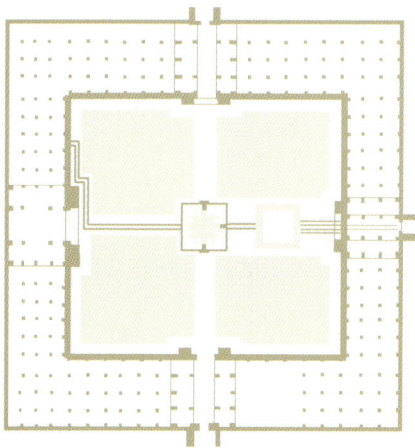

facing page, left. Mosque of Shah Hamadan, Srinagar, Kashmir.

above. Layout plan of the Jami Masjid, Srinagar, Kashmir.

top. Sketch depicting the Jami Masjid, Srinagar, Kashmir.

the outer surface is virtually a rooftop garden containing beds of tulip and iris, a truly fabulous sight during the spring.

The most striking feature of the Shah Hamadan Masjid is the use of four grand wooden pillars, nearly 7m in height, forming a square bay at the centre. The interior contains eight sided pillars, with foliated bases and capitals, the arched and recessed mihrab, panelled walls and floor covered with exquisite carpets. The whole architectural style of this seventeenth century mosque is functional and non-fussy.

Besides these two mosques built in wood, the only other structure of any importance is the tomb of Zainul Abidin's mother (c.1430) built over the ruins of a dismantled temple. The present brick superstructure is topped by a central dome surrounded by four smaller corner domes. Each side of the structure has a pointed-arch opening. This brick structure shows a strong Persian influence.

The tomb of Haji Muhammad Sahib has also been built over the ruins of a temple. The tomb and mosque of Madani (c.1444) in Zadibal, however, retains much more of the original temple structural material in its present fabric. The timber architectural style of Kashmir was too deeply rooted in the native, indigenous traditions to allow any form of Persian influence to flourish in the valley, more so in the absence of any major constructions in stone.

The Mughals, never short of manpower and resources, built in their typical grand style creating a majestic setting befitting rulers of a great kingdom. Akbar built the Hari Parbat fort overlooking the Dal Lake. Only two gateways have survived Kathi Darwaza and Sangin Darwaza. There are no great palaces within since the fort is a mere skeleton of a defence structure at

Tomb of Rukn-i Alam in Multan, Pakistan

this mountainous outpost of the Mughal Empire. Nurjahan built the Patthar Masjid in 1623. The Akhun Mulla Shah Masjid was built in 1649. These two mosques follow the conventional mosque style with little to distinguish them in either architectural splendour or elegance of embellishment. At the Akhun Mulla Shah Masjid the sanctuary stands detached in a square courtyard as an independent structure. The ablution tank and cloistered rooms for visitors are a part of the general scheme marked with an overall simplicity of style. The arches are particularly graceful. The Mughal architectural style, known for its splendour and marble work, is singularly rudimentary and functional in Srinagar. The pavilions in the Shalimar and the Nishat gardens, except for the magnificent backdrop of mountains and streams, are rather common place architectural adjuncts.

MULTAN AND LAHORE

Both Multan and Lahore, now in Pakistan, were the earliest cities in the Indian territory to come in contact with Islam. Multan was the first city to experience Muslim rule in India. It was thrice conquered by the Arabs in the eighth and ninth centuries. During 879-980 Multan was the capital of the Arab state, later passing into the hands of Karmatians the Ghaznavids, the Ghurids and finally assimilated into the Delhi Sultanate by Iltutmish. For nearly seventy five years between 1457 and 1525, Multan was ruled by the Langhas.

Surprisingly Multan has very few monuments of any real historical or architectural significance. A mosque with minarets was built here in 712 but it has completely disappeared. There are five tombs of saints, which are of considerable architectural significance. Two of these tombs have been altered extensively during repairs. The tomb of Shah Yusuf Gardizi (1152), earliest of the group, is a flat roofed, rectangular structure standing within an enclosed area. The exterior is mostly plain unbroken surface except for slight projections over the entrance and the back of the western wall where the position of the mihrab inside is indicated by a projection outside. The whole structure is covered with encaustic tiles mostly carrying geometrical designs.

The tomb of Bahaul Haqq (1262) was the work of the saint himself. The other tomb of Shamsuddin (1276) is locally known as Shams-i-Tabrizi. Both the monuments are built on a similar architectural plan-a single square tomb chamber with battered walls surmounted by a lofty octagon and a hemispherical dome to form a uniform structural pattern for this group of tombs. The receding planes of the central arched entrance at the Shah Bahaul Haqq tomb is the only striking feature on the tall 40 feet height of the square base. The battlemented parapet provides a little relief from the starkness of the lower portion. The arched openings on each face of the octagonal section form the clerestory below the dome.

It is, however, the tomb of Rukn-i-Alam, the grandson of Bahaul Haqq, which remains the most perfect and splendid example of tombs built in Multan. It was built by Ghiyasuddin

Tughlaq for himself between 1320 and 1324 but subsequently went on to house the mortal remains of the saint. The structure has an impressive height of 35m and its diametre is 29m. It is an octagonal structure with buttressed outer quoins with engaged and tapering turrets. The structure has been further strengthened by inserting carved planks of timber into the walls at regular intervals. The brickwork is extremely refined and chiselled. The blue and white tiles covering large sections of the structure are still elegant. The architectural style of this tomb assimilating strains of three cultures-Arabian, Persian and Indian went on to formulate the architectural style of the Tughlaqs in Delhi.

Other examples of brick and stone architecture from the Sind province are seen at Thatta. The tomb of Jam Nizamuddin (1509) is square in plan and covered with profuse carving on stone. The tomb of Isa Khan Tarkhan (1644) has the central square chamber surrounded by a double storeyed verandah. The surface ornament resembles work at Fatehpur Sikri. Among the brick tombs is the tomb of Amir Khalil (1580). It is externally octagonal but square internally, with deeply recessed half-domed arches in sides and a pointed dome in Persian style. The two-tier dome on a circular drum at the tomb of Jani Beg (1599) is also Persian in inspiration. The minar, near the tomb of Mir Muhammad Masum in Sukkur (1594) is built in four stages in a circular form slightly tapering towards the top. The Jami Masjid at Thatta, built in 1657 is a massive brick structure built on a conventional plan of a courtyard surrounded by cloisters. The distance from Multan and Thatta to the Imperial capital was too much for any inspiration from architectural trends in Delhi to take roots in this far-away sandy tract and create structures of any distinction.

If Multan and Thatta show a strong Persian influence on indigenous architecture, Lahore shows yet another source of inspiration, if not exactly influence. Lahore was invaded by both Mahmud Ghazni and Muhammad Ghori from Afghanistan, and was for sometime the capital of the much shrunken Ghaznavide kingdom. Almost all structural remains of this 11th- 12th century period have been destroyed.

Some rare specimens of wooden doors of Ghaznavide-Saljuqian origin can still be observed in Lahore. The wood used is the 'ber' variety. The carving, with its immense projecting bosses, is typically Saljuqian. In the absence of suitable stone for construction, brick, reinforced by wooden beams, was the most preferred material for building. This also explains the absence of arches in structures which were battered in the style of tents for stability and strength. The doors and small windows acquire greater importance in the general architectural scheme. The whole structure is covered with plaster and decorated with encaustic tiles. The carving on doors resembles heavy decorative tassels and knotted fringes on tents. The inhabitants of Punjab and the invaders who spent considerable lengths of time, living in a nomadic lifestyle in deserts, designed their buildings and the decoration therein after a mode of existence familiar to them for centuries in the past.

5

BENGAL
THE ILYAS SHAHI &
THE HUSSAIN SHAHI RULERS

It is a little surprising that the beginnings of a provincial style of Indo-Islamic architecture should have been made in Bengal, within ten years of the founding of the Delhi Sultanate in 1192. The relentless impetuosity with which the Turkish forces raced to the eastern boundaries of the country showed their determination to conquer the land and expand their territories. The Quwwat-ul-Islam mosque had just been completed and the Qutb Minar stood only in its first uncompleted stage. There was no established architectural style at the Imperial capital. In 1204 Ikhtiyar Khilji, another general of Muhammad Ghori's army, surprised Lakshmansena of Bengal at Nadia and established his own rule although nominally under the Delhi Sultanate. Bengal became fully independent of the Imperial yoke during the rule of Muhammad Tughlaq. In 1576 Bengal was assimilated into the Mughal kingdom.

The Islamic architecture of Bengal can be conveniently divided into three phases: first, from 1204 to 1340 when the capital was at Lakhnauti, later called Gaur; second, from 1340 to 1425 when the capital was at Pandua; and third, from 1425 to 1576 when the capital moved back to Gaur. The distance of 27 km between the two centres was never too much for swift movement of the troops and people. The Ganges and the Mahananda rivers fed the land, which had rains and floods in plenty.

Tribeni provides two examples of early architecture in Bengal. A much dilapidated mosque here carries an inscription dated 1298. The tomb of Zafar Khan Ghazi is clearly a Krishna temple suitably altered to function as a tomb chamber. Brickwork walls containing pointed arches illustrate the necessity of resorting to local building material in fashioning new structures. The rulers were in no hurry to force Islamic conventions on the people, or build structures as symbols of the new political power. A general tolerance and liberal attitude characterised the Ilyas Shahi and Hussain Shahi rulers of Bengal.

The earliest specimen of Islamic architecture in Pandua is a severely damaged mosque. Its walls and arches are made of brick and the pillars are in basalt. A portion of the central aisle and the pulpit in carved stone still stands amid sheer ruins. A much later structure is an impressive tower, built towards 1340. The only notable features of this victory tower are the faces and flanges decorating the upper storeys, not ruling out the inspiration it derived from the Qutb Minar.

The new rulers readily accepted the tradition on brickwork as essential to the new architectural projects. Bengal has the richest and most sophisticated heritage of building in bricks and decoration in terracotta. Persia and Iraq provide the earliest

Firoz Minar, Gaur

facing page. Tomb of Fateh Khan, Gaur

examples of notable brick structures outside India. The Gupta period ruins in India also contain remarkable examples of brickwork and chiseling wall surfaces. Also, pointed arches of small dimensions constructed on the corbel system were not unknown to Bengal in the pre-Muslim days. The Muslim rulers built on these two indigenous traditions in brickwork and terracotta decoration. Most of these early structures were allowed to decay and their ruins perhaps still lie under mounds of earth littered around Gaur and Pandua covered with wild proliferating vegetation in the deltic region.

The finest example of Islamic architecture in Bengal appeared only in 1364 when Sikandar Shah built the Adina Masjid at Pandua. It is a huge and magnificent structure by its size alone. Its outer dimensions being approximately 155m by 87m, large enough to accommodate thousands of people at prayer. The courtyard is spectacular, surrounded by a three bay deep corridor on the east. North and south sides and five bay deep on the western side. Considerable portions of the mosque have collapsed but much remains to testify its original grand planning.

The courtyard lies between 260 pillars and 88 archways on all sides with each bay covered by a dome, to number nearly 306 in all. The exterior, in the absence of any lofty entrance gateway, looks massive but monotonous.

The roofless nave has received utmost attention. The front entrance of the central pointed arch, the flanking smaller arches, and the massive brick-worked arched vault over the nave collapsed long ago leaving it exposed to the elements. Over the mihrab can be seen some splendid decoration-large rosettes and an interlaced ornamental device. The northern portion of the sanctuary contains an upper story, a compartment for royal visitors called Badshah ka takht (seat of the king). It is supported on heavy piers surmounted by massive bracket pillars. The pillars actually used in the upper gallery are graceful and fluted in form. The whole western wall contains thirty two mihrabs. The arches and domes are built in brick but the substructure is made of basalt masonry. Almost all pillars have been obtained from pre-Muslim period ruins.

The mihrab is also noteworthy for its 'drop' arch with its centre at the import level and its span greater than its radii. Another important feature of the arches at this mosque is the use of pendentives formed of brick built in over sailing courses with corners of the bricks sticking out in the 'stage of transition' from square to circular.

The Adina Masjid is the largest building at Pandua. At first glance its dimensions have an overwhelming effect on the viewer but at closer observation the monotonous appearance of long ranges of similar looking archways asserts itself. The architecture, in parts, looks perfect but lacks organic composition. It might have served better as a place for vast congregations. As a mosque it looks rather commonplace. As Sir Wolseley Haig sternly observes: "Surely no place of worship was ever devised of such magnitude and with so little sense for the beautiful". The Adina Masjid is singularly lacking in imagination and that harmonious blending of parts so very crucial to the creation of real beauty in architecture.

The only other contemporary structure of some merit is the Kotwali Darwaza at Gaur. The projecting turrets flanking the archway taper toward the top in the Tughlaq style. The mosque and the tomb of Akhi Surajuddin have undergone too much and frequent alterations to give any clear idea of the original conception.

The third phase of architectural activity in Gaur and Pandua shows, as Percy Brown remarks, that "the country originally possessed by the invaders now possessed them". The new Islamic architecture adopted the curved cornice, used over huts and carriages in the rural country to drain off excessive water of the roof. This curved cornice soon become an ubiquitous part of the architectural medium in Bengal. The soil in this deltaic region lacks firmness. Riverbeds keep shifting; banks are eroded;

facing page, above. Badshah ka Takht, Pandua   *above. The Adina Mosque in Pandua*   *below. Bada Sona mosque*

watercourses get silted; and inundation during the rainy season is only normal. Also shortage of stone supply, once the period of using templestones in new construction was over, postulated building in the indigenous tradition to wood and bamboo. If the buildings in Gaur and Pandua are small and unpretentious, it is because the use of wood and mud rendered impossible the effects of spaciousness created by the arch, vault and the dome. Also, perhaps the want of firmness in the soil thwarted desire to build heavy structures in stone which, in any case was only scarcely available from distant quarries.

The Ekalakhi tomb, belonging to Sultan Jalauddin Muhammad Shah (1414-1431) is the first example of the mature architectural style in Pandua. It is a simple square chamber nearly 7.5m high with a triple curved cornice surmounted by a hemispherical dome and octagonal turrets at the four corners. The facade divided by string courses is decorated with ornamental panels. The doorways have been procured from Hindu structures but a pointed arch has been installed over the top beam to create the Islamic appearance. But dependence on the wood and brick architecture had its own limitations-it gave little scope to experiment with form and style. Still, the Ekalakhi tomb has the finest and most sophisticated brickwork in this part of the country. If the Ekalakhi tomb suffers in comparison with the tomb of Rukn-i-Alam in Multan or the Sayyid monuments in

Delhi, it is because it lacks the height and dignity so essential to monumental structures. The care lavished upon surface decoration at the tomb is disproportionate to the care for structural grandeur.

Dakhil Darwaza (c.1465) built by Barbak Shah (1459-74) is the most impressive gateway to the citadel of Gaur. An arched passage with rooms for security guards on both sides runs through this massive structure. The rounded bastions on its corners and pylon-like buttresses on both sides of the high entrance arch lend it a look of magnificence. Most of the superstructure has now disappeared. The facade is variegated with turrets and bastions. Terracotta decoration consists of such motifs as rosettes, flaming suns, hanging lamps, fretted borders and sunken arches. The classic simplicity of the structure gains immensely from the high standard of brickwork. The Dakhil Darwaza, abandoned to the cruel elements and tropical overgrowth for long, has yet survived because of its solid strength.

The architecture of the mosque was governed by the rigours of rain and humidity. The open courtyard was found to be of little use in a country where it either rained incessantly for days or the overpowering heat compelled people to run for cover and shade. The most favoured design for the mosque was the closed or covered design-generally a rectangular or oblong structure with a facade formed by a range of pointed arches shaded by the curved cornice, and projecting octagonal turrets at the corners. The rectangular panels covered with lavish ornamentation in terracotta work on the facade contributed considerable beauty and splendour to the modest structures. Small hemispherical domes over each bay in the sanctuary, and pendentives of bricks resembling a simplified stalactite vaulting are most frequently used. The mihrabs are elaborately decorated.

The Tantipara Masjid at Gaur (1475) has a long rectangular facade formed by five pointed archways. The decoration in floral patterns is extremely rich. The low relief work on the exterior is rather too delicate. Despite the pernicious effect of rain and sun on the exposed portions the splendour of ornament has survived. The Darasbari Masjid (1480) is particularly rich in terracotta decoration which also contains the famous 'palm and parasite' motif. Another version of this theme appears at the jali screen at Sidi Aayyid Masjid in Ahmedabad.

The Chota Sona Masjid (1510), built by Wali Muhammad Khan during the reign of Alauddin Husain Khan (1493-1519), has a rectangular sanctuary faced with stone. Rich carving on the curvilinear facade is in the typical Bengal style. The use of multi-cusped arches on the five-arched openings creates a distinctive façade. The Bara Sona Masjid (1526) has eleven arches on its twelve-door façade. It is a multi-domed structure with massive entrance gateways on the east, north and south sides. The interior is three bay deep, with a verandah in the front. Originally there were forty four domes on the roof. Now, in absence of the ceiling over the sanctuary which has collapsed, only eleven domes over the verandah ceiling have survived.

The Chamkatti Masjid (1575) in Gaur is a square brick chamber with stone facing in the interior measuring 7m side. The use of glazed tiles is a new feature in decoration though actually it does not contribute much to its beauty. The gabled and curved roof at the small and rectangular tomb of Qadam Rasul (1657) renders the whole structure the look of a thatched hut. It is perhaps the last of the notable buildings in Gaur and Pandua.

The Muslim rulers of Bengal had full opportunities to raise architecture to new high standards. They had a rich heritage of artistry and craftsmanship at their disposal and superior methods of construction to inspire them. Islamic architecture in Bengal could have been great but, somehow, it suffers from a non-progressing, static quality. Excepting the Adina Masjid at Pandua and the Dakhil Darwaza at Gaur, no other structure shows any inspired effort at creating a distinctive architectural style

facing page. Dakhil Darwaza, Gaur
below. Qadam Rasul mosque

6

GUJARAT
THE AHMED SHAHIS

WHEN GUJARAT WAS ANNEXED by Alauddin Khilji to be a part of the Delhi Sultanate in 1298, the architecture of Gujarat under the patronage of the Solanki rulers had already acquired a distinctive character of its own, known far and wide for the exquisitely carved temples at Somnath, Modhera and Mt. Abu. The stonecraft and woodcraft of Gujarat was reckoned as most accomplished in the country. The Khiljis contributed their own sense of symmetry and proportion to the highest aesthetics of architecture acquired by the Gujarati artisan. Working without much interference and absolute encouragement from the new governors of the Sultanate, the artisan and the architect expressed himself with freedom. If the Islamic architecture of Gujarat is called 'the most indigenously India' it is because, excepting the introduction of a few new quintessentially Islamic architectural elements like the dome and arch, it was by and large a continuation of the time-tested, trabeate traditions of Gujarat architecture.

Mosque of Ahmed Shah, Ahmedabad.

In the early phase of Islamic architecture in Gujarat, covering a little more than one hundred years between 1298 and 1411, there emerges the oft-repeated tale of extemporaneous compositions, use of the older site and material for a new purpose. Temples built by rulers of the Solanki and other dynasties were pulled down in assertion of the new power of governors and structures of Islamic character built with the stone so readily obtained from demolition of earlier structures.

The mausoleum of Sheikh Farid at Patan (1300) is among the earliest few structures of the Muslim rule in Gujarat. It was an ancient temple suitably altered to function as the tomb of the saint. The Jami Masjid at Patan (1300) is a new orderly rearrangement of nearly one thousand temple pillars. The whole structure was hastily put together and crumbled soon thereafter to leave behind only foundations indicating the mosque plan.

The Jami Masjid at Broach is an open-pillared mosque. The pillars are richly carved and retain their original brackets which once supported the mandapa ceilings. Cusped and geometrical patterns on square, sunk coffered ceilings and the pillars retain their original character. The walls of the mosque evidence some deliberate planning, particularly the mihrabs and the arched windows on the western side. The inclusion of the pointed arch has been fastidiously adhered to in compliance with the new order.

The arch screen in front of the pillared sanctuary appears at the Jami Masjid at Cambay (1325), in clear evidence of the inspiration derived from the Quwwat-ul-Islam Mosque at the Qutb Minar and the Jamat Khana Masjid at Nizamuddin in Delhi. Also noteworthy is the introduction of an engrailed arch standing under the central arched entrance to the sanctuary. Blocks of jali screens cover windows on the western wall to provide light without glare in the interior. Two small ornamental turrets atop the parapet over the central arch, are, however, too diminutive in size to be of any particular consequence to the architectural scheme at this stage.

The mosque of Hilal Khan in Dholka (1333) is noteworthy for the use of tall, ornamental turrets on both sides of the central archway, and also for one pillared canopy at each corner. The pulpit is one of the finest of its kind at this stage. The new architectural elements are far from being perfect and a certain awkwardness and tentativeness in the effort is all too apparent. The Tanka Masjid here (1361) is an open pillared mosque making good use of richly carved pillars. There is no effort to introduce any new architectural feature. It is a purely functional structure, built to meet the demands of a rising Muslim population.

above. Jami Masjid, Ahmedabad.
facing page, top left. The Tree of Life as decorative element at the Jami Masjid.   right. Corbelled dome and balconies of Jami Masjid.
bottom left. Interior of Jami Masjid.   right. Jali work at the Shah Alam Rauza

These mosques at Patan, Broach, Cambay and Dholka provide the earliest examples of Islamic architecture in Gujarat, built not in pursuance of high architectural ideals but only as symbols of the new change in political and religious authority. The artisans were no longer bound by injunctions of the *shilpashastras*, instead enjoyed a complete freedom in executing works explained to them by word of mouth only. The seat of the Khilji and Tughlaq sultans was far away in Delhi. The artisans depended on their own unrivalled aesthetic resources and architectural achieve. As Percy Brown explains: "Although in every intention strictly Islamic, the pattern of these buildings, or what may be called the undertones, are in the idiom of the country while, … in some of the finer examples considerable portions of their compositions are adaptations and even entire extracts from either Hindu or Jain temples…in this instance the

artisans were probably more resourceful, more fertile, and more vitally the artistic than elsewhere". The architecture during the first phase of its beginning in the fourteenth century offers greater confirmation of the artisan's inherent talent and mastery of the trabeate system than the arcuate style of Islamic architecture. The excellence accomplished in chiselling sculptured facades on temples creates opportunities for a similar display on the mosque facades in a nearly uninterrupted continuation of the earlier architectural tradition.

The second phase of the Islamic architectural activity in Gujarat was ushered in by Ahmad Shah I (1411-1442) who founded the new capital city of Ahmedabad in 1411. He inaugurated a continued building programme which ultimately included nearly fifty mosques, big and small, and a few tombs besides the building of the Bhadra citadel in the heart of the city

over the Sabarmati river. This group of monuments, mostly mosques, forms the most formidable exposition of Islamic architecture in the region.

The mosque of Sayyid Alam (1412) is amongst the first few mosques completed during the reign of Ahmad Shah I. It is notable chiefly for features which were to evolve later into graceful architectural elements. The minars (now without turrets), the triple arched entrances of equal height, the higher stilted central wing rising above the lower-roofed side wings and the solitary buttress at the back of the central mihrab contribute to the elegance of this mosque. The provision for an additional intermediate storey or embryo triforium in the nave shows a step towards improving the interior of the mosque.

The mosque of Ahmad Shah (1414) was the royal chapel. It has a screen of five arches in front of the sanctuary. The ten large domes interspaced with smaller domes give it a dignified look. The sanctuary which is three bay deep, contains 152 pillars and eight windows covered with perforated screens. The zenana enclosure is on the northwest corner. The central mihrab has a black and white marble casing. The small platform, meant for the sultan, is situated in front of this mihrab. The pillars in the sanctuary and the ring-dome structure are all obtained from demolished structures. This is the first big mosque in Ahmedabad which underlines the difficulty in creating screen of arches here separated by wide stretches of solid wall and small, insignificant looking windows. The central arched entrance to the sanctuary is flanked by quasi buttresses. Two elegantly carved pillars joined by a beam form yet another architectural element of typical temple origin.

The mosque of Haibat Khan (1412) has a pair of tapering turrets on the front and the exterior of the western wall has five rounded bastions in the Tughlaq tradition. The tapering turrets indicate the desire to experiment with the form later culminating

in the elegant minars. The pillars and the domed ceilings are richly carved, particularly the central dome with its pendentive carving so reminiscent of the Dilwara ceilings at Mt. Abu.

The Teen Darwaza, a splendid structure of a different kind, is a magnificent triple-arched gateway, built on the royal processional route issuing from the Bhadra citadel. It belongs to the earliest years of the Ahmad Shahi rule. It is not a mammoth creation, only 37 feet in height and 80 feet in width. The pointed arches topped by three oriel windows on brackets and the richly carved buttressed piers are extremely impressive.

The Jami Masjid (1423) is amongst the finest mosques in the country. It has a spacious flagged courtyard (75m by 66m) surrounded by a single arcade on the east, north and south sides. The sanctuary has a well-proportioned arched facade combining two different conventions-screen of arches and pillared portico. Here the screen of arches is placed at the centre with the pillared portico on the wings. The volume and strength of the massive wall surface and the airy lightness of the colonnade creates an effective composition of solids and voids. The central arch is flanked by lavishly sculptured lower portions of truncated towers, typical of the Jain and Brahmanical temples. The two smaller side arches are set within walls of plain stonework with minimum decoration except niches carved on both sides. The niches on the walls filled up with exquisitely carved jali screens, instead of containing images of deities as done at the temples, merely replicate the architectural element of the traditional Hindu places of worship. On both north and south sides are rows of five stilted columns with elegant brackets. The facade shows a clear progression in height from the trabeated single storeyed bays of the wings to the intermediate arches onto the prominent area of the central nave corresponding to three storeys.

The interior of the Jami Masjid shows a fascinating

above. Tomb of saint Makhdum Shah Ahmad Khattu, Sarkhej.   facing page. Mosque at Sarkhej.

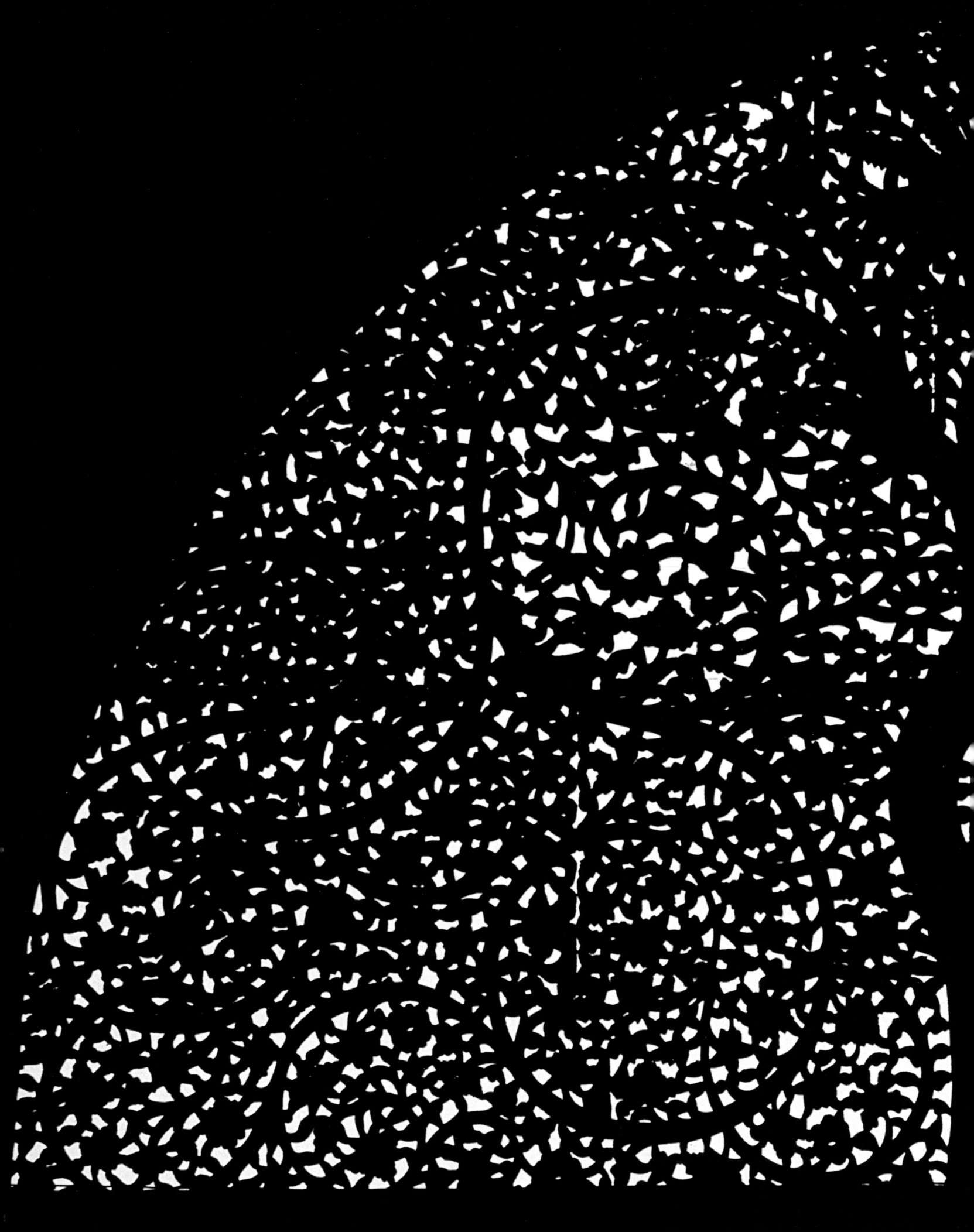

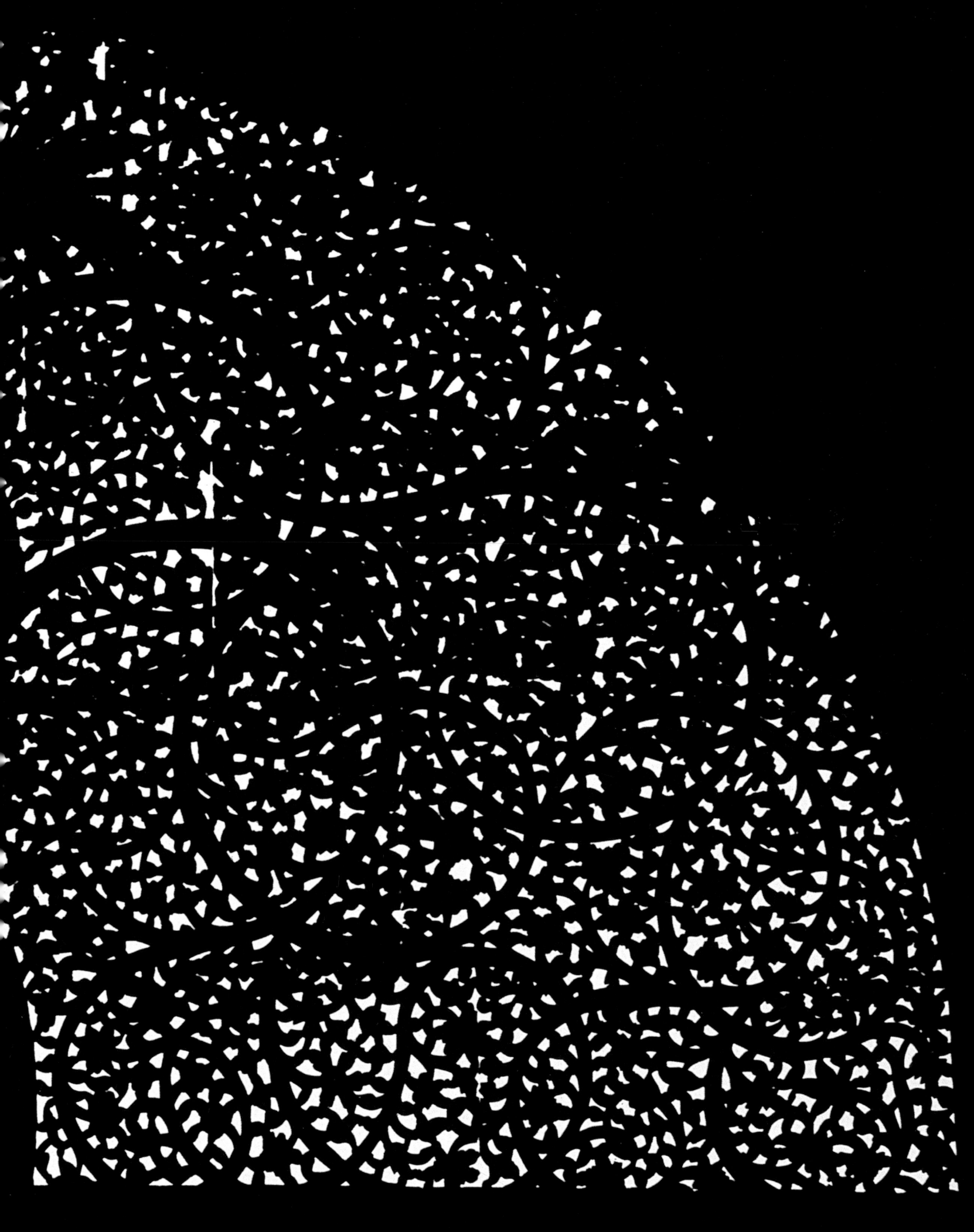

arrangement of nearly 260 richly carved temple pillars of varying size. The inter-columniation is less than five feet but little wider at the nave over which the architects have scientifically provided an ingenious system of mezzanines, forming two pillared galleries one above the other, enclosing the central area topped by a corbelled dome. These balconies have seats with back rests (asanas) as seen at the temples, and clerestories filled with jali screens to admit light. Herein, the use of pillars emerges into an established architectural order which also solves the problem of better illumination in the interior and the necessity of increasing the height of the domed ceiling over the nave to accommodate the two mezzanines.

The exquisitely carved cusped arch rising over tall, slender columns, set up behind the central entrance shows the compulsions of the Gujarati artisan failing to comprehend the dichotomy on the all-Hindu architectural elements proliferating under the shadow of the Islamic pointed arch. The whole setting resembles a temple *torana* and *mandapa* transplanted into a foreign territory

The Jami Masjid, despite the all-too-apparent flaws inherent in the Islamic project executed in the Hindu style, shows a nearly perfect symbiosis of the two vastly different architectural traditions. The high and pointed central arch ensconced between lavishly sculptured turrets (their upper portions destroyed by an earthquake in 1819) looks magnificent and majestic.

The tomb of Ahmad Shah lies close to the Jami Masjid. In a nearby enclosed area called Rani ka Hazira, lie the tombs of queens. These tombs are built close to the eastern entrance to the great mosque.

The architectural style in most of the mosques and tombs built around the middle of the fifteenth century shows no marked change or progress. Only two noteworthy structures appeared in Sarkhej near Ahmedabad. The tomb of the famous saint Makhdum Sheikh Ahmad Khattu (1336-1445) is the most important structure of its kind and the open-pillared mosque here is a really splendid example of mosque architecture. Begun in 1446, both these structures were completed during the

previous pages. 'Tree of Life' from the Sidi Sayyid Mosque, Ahmadabad.

below. Detail of Minar from the Rani Sipri mosque in Ahmadabad.

reign of Ahmad Shah II (1451-1458).

The tomb rises over a plinth area of 31.70m square. The façade contains nine arches of varying sizes. The portion of walls over these arches is filled with perforated screens in square panels creating the impression of a double storey. The interior is partitioned by screen panels in brass and stone. It is the largest tomb in Gujarat. The structure is toped by a huge impressive dome surrounded by rows of smaller domes.

The mosque at Sarkhej has a large, spectacular courtyard measuring 399.48 sq.m. including the sanctuary. There are nearly one hundred and twenty pillars in the sanctuary lying under a flat roof crowned with five large and forty smaller domes symmetrically rising over the pillared squares in the sanctuary. The chaste simplicity of style of this mosque has a classic elegance. There is no arch screen and minars have found no place in the architectural scheme of the mosque. "The mosque is the perfection of elegant simplicity and is an improvement on the plan of the Jami Masjid... Except the Moti Masjid at Agra", observes James Fergusson, "these is no mosque in India more remarkable for simple elegance than this".

Sarkhej became the centre of immense architectural activity during the reign of Mahamud Begada(1458-1511) the greatest of Gujarat sultans, when palaces, tombs and gardens were built here around the large artificial lake. The Gujarat architecture reached its zenith under this ruler who founded three cities-Mustafabad at Junagarh, Mahmudabad near Ahmedabad, and Muhammadabad at Champaner. The trabeate style of construction continued to be in use prominently though the arch-and-vault of the arcuate method also firmly emerged out of the preliminary tentative use.

The mosque in the Rajapur suburb of Ahmedabad (1454) was built for Sayyid Buddha bin Sayyid Yaqut, mother of Ahmad Shah II. It is a rather heavy and ponderous structure with a triple-arched façade. The minars flanking the central arch are exceptionally rich in sculptural ornamentation. The minars rise in three storeys marked by three exquisite balconies supported by heavy brackets. The conical top, however, adds little to the splendour of these minars. In 1819 an earthquake destroyed the upper section of the southern minar.

It was about this time that two structures were built entirely in bricks, a rare feature of architecture in Gujarat. Both Darya Khan's tomb in Ahmedabad and the mosque of Alif Khan in Dholka make good use of arches and heavy brick piers without recourse to pillar and beam. The inspiration for these brick structures was perhaps derived from the contemporary architecture of Southern Persia. Stone, however, continued to be the preferred material for construction in Gujarat.

The long reign of Mahmud Begada is also responsible for providing greater acceptability of the *rauza*, building tomb and the accompanying mosque as a combined architectural project. In such arrangements, the mosque is generally of the open-pillared variety. The *rauza* of Sayyid Usman at Usmanpura(1460) is not distinguished for any particular feature except the two six-storeyed minarets at both ends of the pillared sanctuary. The two

mosques-of Mian Khan Chist (1456) and of Bibi Achut Kuki (1472), however, show a definite progress toward elimination of pillars in the side wings of the arched facade and the extension of the screen of arches to cover the entire length of the front.

The *rauza* of Shah Alam(1475) reveals another aspect of the Ahmad Shahi rulers - their great reverence for the establishment of Sayyids or Darvishes founded by Burhanuddin and his successors. The tomb of Muhammad Shah Alam follows a casket-like arrangement with a large traceried compartment enclosing another traceried compartment containing the cenotaph at the centre. There is an all too noticeable greater reliance on the use of pointed arches and the arcuate system in general for greater flexibility and enhanced strength of the building. The elegantly designed perforated screens fully covering space between pillars contributes that element of exquisite craftsmanship for which the Gujarati architecture is justly known far and wide, and from which the classic and chaste simplicity of the true Islamic style could never entirely redeem itself in Gujarat.

The mosque of Muhafiz Khan (1492) is a small gem of architecture, noted for its facade design which contains only three arched openings and no side wings. The extravagantly carved minars are at the extreme ends of the facade. These minars carry in-built flight of steps to the top. The entrance to the steps is provided from the inner wall face. The mosque at the *rauza* of Rani Rupavati, built during the reign of Muzaffar Shah I (1511-1526) is yet another beautiful structure covered with typically Gujarati sculptural decoration of a high order. The two balcony windows on each side of the smaller arches add immense variety to the facade. The turrets flanking the central arch are exceptionally rich in sculptural detail. The portion over the nave is raised a storey above the flanks, functioning as the clerestory upholding the dome. This mosque has the richest surface decoration.

Rani Sipri Mosque (1514) rivals the Rani Rupavati Mosque in beauty. It is noteworthy for the placement of the two slender minarets at either end of the pillared facade. There are no in-built steps within the minar structure. The blending of various architectural parts is here most perfect and harmonious. The open pillared facade of the prayer hall, unbroken line of eaves-board or *chajja*, equal height of cornice and crenellated corona over it, stone tracery windows and the four-storeyed slender minarets-all these elements contribute greatly to the charm of this mosque.

The small mosque at Isanpur (1525) has an elegant facade with three central openings. It contains the unique example of a cusped arch used at the central entrance, a feature which fascinated the Mughals who used it as indispensable to their architecture.

Sidi Sayyid's Mosque is almost the last great mosque in Ahmedabad. It belongs to the last year of the independent Gujarat Sultanate. It was constructed between 1572-1573 by Sheikh Said, a prominent noble at the time of Muzaffar III(1561-1573). The prayer hall has a facade of five well proportioned

arches with a deep cornice above supported on brackets. The arches in the hall spring from tall square stone piers, instead of pillars and beams. Each of the fifteen bays supports the vaulted lower part of the flat ceiling above in three different pendentive systems of bracket, diagonal beam and squinch.

Sidi Sayyid's Mosque has acquired a world-wide fame for the incredible superior craftsmanship lavished on the carving of the jali screens covering the tympana. The filigree work-like delicacy and the unerring sense of rhythm displayed on particularly two central screens depicting the 'tree of life' and 'palm and parasite' motifs remains unequalled by any other specimen of jali work in India or abroad. Even the Mughals failed to achive anything approaching these panels in the felicity of lyrical expression creating vegetal forms in such conventionalized yet tremendously fascinating manner.

The monuments belonging to the later part of Mahmud Begada's reign include his mausoleum and palaces built on the edge of the lake at Sarkhej. His greatest contribution to architecture in Gujarat, however, can be seen at Champaner where he built a citadel with massive gateways and bastions, the Shihr-ki-Masjid, the Nagina, the Kevda, the Khajuri and the Ek-Minar Masjid and many other splendid structures in a uniformly superior standard.

The Jami Masjid at this forgotten capital of the Gujarat Sultanate remains the most outstanding achievement of mosque architecture in the state. Three impressive gateways fitted with square panels of exquisitely fashioned perforated screens provide entrance to the mosque. These gateways add an elegance and splendour independent of the general structure of the mosque contained within the walled enclosure.

The sanctuary has a facade of five pointed archways with the central arch flanked by two slender minarets carrying decoration limited to the lower portions only. Clearly enough, the zeal and predilection towards sumptuous ornamentation in imitation and continuation of similar work at Jain and Brahmanical temples lost its fervour at this new city. The sanctuary is a pillared hall containing 176 pillars with the nave in three storeys. Much planning and effort has apparently been bestowed on this part of the mosque, designed to improve deliberately upon the nave at

Jami Masjid in Ahmedabad. Access to each upper floor is available from the staircases built within the minarets. With the top balcony nestling under the ribbed dome immediately above it, there are stone seats provided for those given to meditation in isolation. The whole arrangement of pillars and the rising sroreys over the nave, somehow, looks slightly cramped, leaving no space between the nave and the transepts. Most significantly, even at this advanced stage of Islamic architecture in the state, the trabeate system continues to hold on relentlessly to the building scheme. The arch and the dome have been assimilated into the architectural scheme in a gesture of stoic submission to the patron's orders.

The minarets at the Champaner Jami Masjid, built in six stages, indicate a fleeting phase of Islamisation of surface ornamentation as seen at most of the mosques in Ahmedabad. Here the upper five storeys are rather plain except for the heavily sculptured brackets in a marked difference from the minarets in Ahemedabad where the profundity of sculptural detail cuts across the need for restained decoration and classic simplicity the ideals of Islamic architecture. However, the built-in steps within the minar structure, seem to have gained wide acceptance as the norm.

The shaking minarets at Sidi Bashir's mosque and Bibi ki Masjid have remained an unexplained architectural phenomenon. These minarets have three balconies above the parapet and are nearly 21.34m high. Architects and scientists have studied the techniques of construction employed to produce this effect. However, since this effect was noticed only in the eighteenth century, it is believed to have been caused by the decaying process affecting the stones and the binding material. When the top most part of the minaret is slowly shaken from the third balcony, the shaking effect gradually gathers momentum and travels downward, through the terrace, to the central arch reaching the other minaret and shaking it gradually but visibly. Perhaps this effect is caused by the employment of a particular stone for foundation-cushioning in both the minarets by which the movement locally imparted in one limb is reacted upon the other. The bridge connecting the two minarets acts in unison for creating this swinging effect.

left. Champaner Jami Masjid.

7

JAUNPUR
THE SHARQIS

Jaunpur, about 60 kilometres from Varanasi, was the capital of a small kingdom ruled over by the Sharqis between 1360 and 1480. Malik Sarwar, a eunuch in Muhammad Tughlaq's household and titled Khwaja Jahan, was appointed governor of this small provincial kingdom, wedged between Delhi and Bengal. Malik Sarwar was now titled Maliku'sh Sharq (King of the East). In 1394, he claimed independence to found his own dynastic rule Sharqis of Jaunpur, which lasted for nearly 85 years till overcome by the forces of Bahlol Lodi. It was Sikandar Lodi who finally destroyed the Sharqis towards the end of the fifteenth century. It was under Ibrahim Shah Sharqi (1402-1436) that Jaunpur rose to eminence attracting poets, artists and craftsmen from Delhi. The decline of the Tughlaqs and their ultimate disintegration following the invasion of Delhi by Timur in 1398 led to the rise of Jaunpur which for its cultural achievements came to be called 'Shiraz of India'. The Lodi rulers never allowed Jaunpur any peace till Sikandar Lodi assimilated this small Kingdom into the Delhi Sultanate.

Almost all monuments of the pre-Sharqi period in Jaunpur have been destroyed leaving behind the skeleton of a fort and a small mosque within its precincts. But the Sharqis built a number of mosques following the great architectural tradition of the Tughlaqs in Delhi and even surpassed in strength, grace and splendour their prototypes in the Imperial capital. The Jaunpur mosques follow an architectural scheme common to most of the Sharqi mosques: tapering minarets, battered sides of the propylons, stucco decoration, arch-and beam openings, and low four-centred arches with decorative fringes all derived from examples of Tughlaq mosques in Delhi and, perhaps built by craftsmen fleeing Delhi for life and work. Timur carried thousands of Delhi craftsmen, stone-cutters and artisans as prisoners to Persia to work there on his buildings. Those craftsmen, who escaped Timur and reached Jaunpur, found ready employment on the Sharqi mosques. Many craftsmen were Hindus who worked on stone ceilings, latticed screens, panels and arches with their tympana carved with floral and geometrical motifs.

The most distinctive feature of the Jaunpur mosques, however, is the tall propylon, a gigantic arch framed within a rectangular frame with much emphasised battered sides. This stupendous structure, functioning as the traditional iwan completely obscures the front view of the massive hemispherical dome built over the sanctuary. In fact, the massive propylon appears to be an architectural element completely independent of the other subsidiary features. The pylon at the Beghumpuri Masjid in Delhi which seems to have inspired the Jaunpur architect is comparatively a modest structure. Still, in its magnificent proportions and splendid exterior decoration, the Jaunpur propylon is an entirely original creation, particularly for the grandeur of the stately arch set within a frame of magnificent towers with buttressed angles.

The Atala Masjid, built in 1408 on the foundations of a temple dedicated to the goddess Atala, earlier destroyed by Firoz Shah Tuglaq in 1376, is the first great Sharqi structure in Jaunpur. It uses up the stone from the pre-Sharqi buildings. The mosque does not stand on a plinth and for this reason alone its facade loses much of the charm and impressive character gained by structures built on a high platform, a feature of prominent Tughlaq mosques. The outer walls at the Atala Masjid have monumental gateways, closely following the design of the propylon on the western wall facing the courtyard. These gateways function as ornamental entrances to the inner precincts. The inner courtyard, 78.7m on a side surrounded by hypo style halls is spectacular. A small ablution tank lies at the centre of the open area.

The most outstanding feature of the whole architectural scheme is the propylon with its two 22.9m high battered towers framing a mammoth recessed arch. The structure has a width of 16.61m across the base and 14.33m at the top showing a batter of 1.13m on either side. The upper section of the arch consists of a double row of five smalls ornamental arch-windows, over and below this double line of arches are other decorative windows. Almost all these arches, big and small, are fringed with stylised spearheads. The main entrance to the sanctuary is a beam-and-lintel opening flanked by two smaller arched entrances. The battered towers, divided through string courses, are decorated with four small sunk arches arranged in a vertical order, on each side. The lower section is severely plain. The whole exterior of the propylon uses the arch, in various shapes and sizes, as a decorative motif, creating the most fascinating facade, remarkable for its balance and rhythm, judicious use of recesses and projections, solids and voids, light and deep shadows. To the right and left of the central propylon stand two smaller propylons of similar design which considerably reduce the disparity between the stupendous height of the propylon and the modest height of the side wings.

facing page. Atala mosque.

right. Madrsa, school for religious learning, part of the mosque complex.

below. Squinch arches in the zone of transition.

facing page. Jami Masjid.

The magnificent dome has a diametre of 16.8m but remains completely hidden behind the gigantic propylon. It is revealed only partially from vantage points below the smaller pylons of entrances on the north and south sides. Perhaps this arrangement of architectural elements-propylon and dome, conforms to contemporary aesthetics in the rest of the Islamic world, notably the Mosque of Bibi Khanum at Samarqand. In its present form at Jaunpur this approach to design remains largely experimental, though stunning in effect.

The sanctuary of the Atala Masjid consists of the nave and wings, each wing comprising an oblong room and two smaller rooms in two storeys in each corner, meant for the ladies. The nave is actually oblong with three mihrabs on the western side and a high pulpit raised on a flight of steps. However, it has been converted into a square by massive corbels projecting from the piers of the side walls. Eight arches, four of which are squinches, form the intermediary stage. These ornamental, fringed arches provide the octagonal base on which the huge hemispherical dome has been raised. The central mihrab has been finished in a splendid style.

The Jami Masjid or Badi Masjid is much larger than Atala Masjid. It is built on a 3.5m high plinth, with a majestic flight of 15 steps to the impressive gateway. It is a grand building and its magnificent proportions reflect the ambitions of its patron Husain Shah (1458-1484), the last Sharqi ruler. Husain Shah made six invasions on Delhi but was either beaten or pushed back or else entered into a truce with Bahlol Lodi, truces which he never kept. His overriding ambition never left him in peace. In 1484, Husain Shah lost Jaunpur finally to Bahlol Lodi, and took shelter in Chunar from where he continued his skirmishes with the Lodis. In 1495, Sikandar Lodi destroyed buildings in Jaunpur, but spared the mosques following protests from the ulama. Husain died in 1505 and the Sharqi rule ended finally.

The propylon at the Jami Masjid is a stupendous creation, measuring 25.70m in height, 23.42m at the base and 21.59m at the top with a batter of 0.94m on either side. This is perhaps the most magnificent entrance to any mosque-sanctuary resembling in its mammoth proportions the gopuram of the temples in southern India. The decoration on the exterior is the finest of its class.

The nave in the central part is covered by a single huge

hemispherical dome crowned by an amalak motif. The clerestory with lattice screens admits light into the interior. The dome, however, has been rendered a redundant structural adjunct, peacefully nestling under the overshadowing upper portion of the propylon. On either side of the nave, placed transversely to the axis of the sanctuary is a long pillared room over which space is provided for a covered galley. On either side is a large barrel-vaulted hall, unsupported by any piers or pillar, measuring 15.01m by 12.07m, and 13.51m in height with three arched openings. An interior with such a large unrestricted area is a rare and unique feature in Indian architecture, a remarkably successful effort at creating a spacious hall for gatherings on special occasions. The imperfections of the front elevation are ascribable to an over ambitious architectural project hastily completed against frequent skirmishes with the Lodi powers constantly harassing the Sharqi ruler, creating a state of constant tension and turmoil in Jaunpur. The tapering turrets on the exterior of the rear western wall create the appearance of a fortified citadel typical of the Tughlaq prototypes.

Whereas the Atala Masjid and the Jami Masjid mark the beginning and the end of the Sharqi rule, three other smaller mosques were built during the intervening period. Maliks Khalis and Mukhlis, two governors of the city, built the Khalis Mukhlis Masjid, popularly known as the Char Angul Ki Masjid, in 1439. It is a functional structure with no attempt at ornamenting the exterior. Its façade, domed interior and transepts follow the same principles of construction as observed at the Atala Masjid.

Built by Ibrahim in honor of Hazrat Sa'id Sadr Jahan Ajmali, the Jhangiri Masjid has survived only in its pylon. The mosque was never completed but the pylon is extremely ornamental with its fragile but elegant lattice-screens on the small arches. The only noteworthy structural feature is the entrance formed by triple openings built on the pillar, lintel-and bracket principle. There are no traces of any subsidiary mosque structure except small portions of a brick wall on the south-eastern corner. The mosque stands amid corn fields overlooking the river Gomti. Perhaps, it was meant to function as an open mosque or Idgah

with the pylon indicating the direction of the Qibla.

The Lal Darwaza Masjid was built in 1450 by Bibi Raji, the queen of Mahmud Shah (1436-1458). It was originally a part of the royal complex. It is a small mosque, nearly two thirds of the Atala Masjid in size. The pylon has a modest height and the courtyard, nearly 40sq.m on a side, has a small ablution tank at the centre. Single-storeyed pillared cloisters surround the courtyard on three sides. The sanctuary measuring 51m by 10.5m also contains screened compartments for ladies. The mosque has only one dome over the sanctuary.

The walls of the Jaunpur fort largely belong to the Sharqi rule. The massive battlemented ramparts and the grand portal were much repaired by Akbar's governor of Jaunpur. A little away from the gate, Munim Khan also built a magnificent gateway as entrance to the enclosure facing the fort. It still retains some of its glazed tile decoration in blue and yellow. The fort today wears a deserted look despite a few structures within its walls.

The mosque within the fort was built by Ibrahim Naik Barbak, brother of Firoz Shah Tughlaq, between 1376-77. It is a modest and simple structure. The sanctuary has three chambers with pillars and flat ceilings. However, the most interesting feature of this unpretentious mosque is a stone column, 8.84m

in height. It stands in the open on the south wing of the mosque. It is square at the base, then octagonal and circular toward the top crowned with an amalak and kalasa motif.

A palace, called *Chihil Sutun* built by Barbak has now completely disappeared. The most outstanding building within the fort is the cluster of Turkish baths with a well-planned arrangement for hot and cold water in its inter-connected domed chambers. It is a rare example of Turkish baths in pre-Mughal times indicating the inspired patronage of the Sharqis.

Munim Khan, Akbar's governor did much to restore the original splendour of Jaunpur, devastated by the Lodis. It is, however, mainly for the bridge over the Gomti river built between 1564 and 1568 still in use that Munim Khan is chiefly remembered today. The bridge has ten arched openings, massive piers with chhattris one on each pier on both sides of the bridge. The Persian inscriptions on the bridge ascribe the bridge to Munim Khan.

Surprisingly, the Sharqi rulers built no monumental tombs for themselves unlike their Tughlaq forbears. They are buried in a small graveyard, close to the northern gateway of the Jami Masjid.

above, left to right. Mosque in the Jaunpur fort.

Turkish baths in the fort.

Gateway, Jaunpur fort.

right. Akbar's bridge on the Gomti river.

8

MANDU
THE GHURI &
THE KHILJI SULTANS

Mandapa Durg, the fort at Mandu, came into prominence in the tenth century with the Gurjara Paratihara and the Paramara rulers who held sway over Malwa. Songarh, a small fortified area with a lake and a few ruined temples still standing on a detached spur of the main plateau, was perhaps the Paramara stronghold in the pre-Muslim period.

Mandu was reduced to a secondary political status when the Paramaras declined in power following three invasions by the Delhi sultans-IItutmish (1227), Jalaluddin Khilji (1293) and later on Alauddin Khilji (1305). However, in 1401 Dilawar Khan, a governor of the Tughlaqs, founded his own independent kingdom in Mandu coinciding with a similar move in Jaunpur where only a little earlier in 1394, Malik Sarwar, governor of the Tughlaqs, claimed independence and founded his own kingdom. Hoshang Shah (1405-53), Dilawar Khan's son shifted capital from Dhar to Mandu in 1405 and ushered in the glorious era of architectural activity. The armies of Humayun (1534), Shershah (1554) and Akbar (1561) finally crushed the spirit of Mandu in the 16th century when Mandu was finally assimilated into the Mughal empire.

The want of any strong local tradition in architecture led the Malwa rulers to look towards the Imperial capital for inspiration. Stone-cutters and masons from Delhi found ready employment with the Malwa rulers to transform their building plans into a reality. The inevitable result of this necessary arrangement was soon apparent in the continuation of chief features of the Tughlaq architecture in an entirely new setting: the arch over the pronounced batter on the outer walls; and a strong inclination

toward using a long and majestic flight of steps as an integral part of the whole architectural scheme. Surely, the Malwa rulers were yet unfamiliar with the splendour of the minaret, conspicuous by its absence on any structure. Buildings are made of grey ashlar covered with plaster. The over-all dullness is only partially relieved by a functional combination of white marble slabs on the pillar-and-lintel. Use of blue and yellow glazed tiles creates a strong and impressive decorative element, still traceable on some structure in Mandu. The palaces, tombs and mosques in Mandu convey the unmistakable impression of a certain ruggedness, vitality and power characteristic of the Tuglaq architecture.

Dhar, ancient capital city of the Paramaras, was also the first capital of the Muslim rulers of Malwa. The Jami Masjid and the Lat Masjid in Dhar belong to the earliest phase of building activity under the new rulers. The Jami Masjid follows the familiar architectural plan of mosques as seen in Delhi. It has a courtyard of 33m north and south by 45m east and west. All the pillars in the mosque have been obtained from ruins of temples and are covered with sculptural decoration typical of the Hindu tradition. The three domes over the sanctuary are modest in height. The screen of arches in front of the is conspicuous by its absence. In fact, the Jami Masjid shows no effort at experimentation.

The Lat Masjid, the other mosque at Dhar, is a small structure. It acquires some importance for the 10m high iron coloumn found here lying in three pieces. It was not originally intended to function as an ornamental adjunct of the temple at the site like the Iron Pillar at the Quwwat-ul-Islam mosque at the

Qutb Minar in Delhi. The Lat Masjid appears impressive as a small and functional structure built before the newly founded kingdom was firmly established at Mandu.

The small fort at Dhar is supposed to have been built by Muhammad Tughlaq and repaired by Dilawar Khan. There is no structure of any significance within the fort.

The Malwa artisans took some care to conceal the sculptural decoration on the pillars by redressing or rubbing down the surface. There is a certain coherence obtained on the exterior. The introduction of a few other architectural features of some notable quality include mention of the interposed pointed arches between the pillars and perforated patterns on the spandrels.

The genius of the Malwa craftsmen revealed itself in full splendour at Mandu. The royal enclosure, near the Alamgiri Gate, contains palaces -Jahaz Mahal, Hindola Mahal, Taveli Mahal, ruins of female quarters, and ornamental pools, baolis and lakes. Jahaz Mahal, the most magnificent and spacious royal place, is an example of elegant and fanciful architecture. The Jahaz Mahal stands ensconced between two splendid lakes- Kapur (camphor) Talao and Munja Talao. Behind the impressive arcaded facade lies the interior comprising three stately halls, subterranean and ante-chambers, pillared compartments all kept cool by water channeled from the two lakes. Though used mostly for lavish royal entertainments, the Jahaz Mahal interior is, by and large, devoid of surface ornamentation. The exterior and the interior are covered with plaster and only sparsely decorated blue tiles. The Jahaz Mahal has massive proportions but appears a light

structure, strong without any heavy solidity. A stately flight of forty five steps leads to the upper terrace lying between two pavilions divided into three compartments, the central one with a domical roof higher that the pyramidal roofs over the side compartments. The small pyramidal roof over a small pavilion projecting over the chief arched entrance below adds variety to the whole architectural scheme. The wide projecting eaves and cornices create a pleasing effect of light and shade.

The two cisterns at the Jahaz Mahal have been most aesthetically designed. Located at the northern end of the structure, on the ground floor and the terrace over it, these pools are carved like lotus. The lower pool is four and a half metres deep with stone steps descending to its depth. A narrow serpentine channel regulates the flow of water supplied through a system of Persian wheels from a tank at the southern end below the steps. The Jahaz Mahal, built by Ghiyasuddin Khilji but sometimes attributed to his predecessor Mahmud, exploits to its fullest advantage its proximity to the water-filled lakes. An octagonal pavilion built over a platform projecting into the Kapur Talao still evokes visions of romantic splendour.

Hindola Mahal (Swing Palace) was built by Hoshang Shah in 1425. It is particularly noteworthy for the awkwardly pronounced batter on its ponderous walls giving it a mammoth, ungainly look. The building is T-shaped with six arch openings on each side. The roofless walls have a thickness of 2.7m. The buttressed strength of walls counteracts the thrust of lofty arches which once supported a massive ceiling. The later additions to the central structure are in the form of brick walled double-storeyed wing for the zenana. In its present form the Hindola Mahal is a mere architectural curiosity owing to the structural transformation it has undergone under the early Ghurid rule at Mandu.

West of the Hindola Mahal lie ruins of the ruler's private residence, some of these belong to remote past but make a truly charming group. Champa Baoli is actually a deep well connected to the palace with subterranean passages and a labyrinth of vaulted rooms comprising the basement. Still in use, the *baoli* lies at the centre of the residential complex which also includes an open entertainment area reserved for the ladies.

Dilawar Khan's mosque is among the earliest buildings in Mandu. It has a central court enclosed by a colonnade, one aisle deep to north, east and south, and four aisles deep on the western side. The pillars and ceilings clearly indicate their Hindu origin. The sanctuary has seven mihrabs with the central one being

prominently lined with black polished stone.

Jal Mahal is a complex of roofless royal residential quarters, believed to have been specially erected for housing the Mughal prince Jehangir and his consort Nurjahan. These most charming ruins stand across the Munja Talao reflecting the magnificent Jahaz Mahal in its entire length. Double-storeyed, and with splendid lotus pools and water tanks it is assumed to be the site where ancient ruins of the Pratihara and Paramara period lie unexcavated under the present charming though dwindling edifices.

Jami Masjid, the impressive congregational mosque was completed by hid successor Sultan Mahmud I in 1440. The mosque covering an area of 85m side is entered through a domed entrance hall standing at the head of a magnificent flight of steps. The lower portions of the front, eastern facade contains a series of arcaded rooms for use as a sarai. The grand courtyard is about 50m square, enclosed on all the four sides by elegant

facing page, and above. The Jama Masjid, Mandu.

arcades of eleven arches. On the northern and southern sides these pillared arcades are three aisles deep. The eastern side is only two aisles deep. The western side containing the sanctuary is five aisles deep. The three large magnificent domes contribute that aura of royal splendour so essential to the most prestigious mosque in Mandu. The entire roof is further covered with one hundred fifty eight small cylindrical cupolas, symmetrically arranged, one over each bay of the interior.

The interior of the sanctuary is virtually made up of arcades of well-proportioned pointed arches covered with minimum decoration. The mihrabs and the mimbar (pulpit) are, however elegantly ornamented. The Jami Masjid is not distinguished by any single outstanding architectural feature. It is in the overall disposition of various structural elements that the solemn grandeur of this mosque reveals itself. According to an inscription the Jami Masjid was designed after the great mosque at Damascus, but actually its main building plan resembles much more the plan of the mosque at Kairwan. The shape of domes at the Jami Masjid resembles the false wooden domes of Palestine and Syria, especially for the false-ribs carved on the domes.

The Asharfi Mahal built by Mahmud I (1436-69) stands in front of the Jami Masjid. Originally, it was meant to house a madarsa. This grand building stands on a high terrace approached by a stately flight of steps, aligned axially with the steps at the mosque. It occupies a square of nearly 100m side and consists of three different structures. The madarsa is built around a rectangular courtyard surrounded by halls and smaller compartments. It had four circular towers at the corners, since destroyed. The corridor of double arches on the front portion of the present basement is all that has survived of the Madarsa structure.

Subsequently the courtyard was filled up and the structure of the grand mausoleum for Mahmud I built on the high plinth. A pillared portico and loggias on each side has survived. The fragmentary ruins of the mausoleum convey, only partially, the impression of grand plans of the structure. White marble was used for decoration on the walls, doorways, windows and cornices etc. Traces of blue and yellow glazed tiles can still be seen at places. The dome must have been larger than the dome of

the Jama Masjid or at the tomb of Hoshang Shah. The interior is 19.9m square. The thickness of walls is 3.4m. The yellow marble base of the sarcophagus still lies exposed to the sun. Despite an ambitious planning, the weak construction caused an early collapse of the supersturcture.

A victory tower commemorating Mahmud Khilji's victory over Rana Kumbha of Chittaurgarh was built at the north-eastern angle of the madarsa building. It is interesting to note that Rana Kumbha also built the splendid Jay Stambha, a victory tower at Chittaurgarh commemorating the same event. The Rajput tower is a grand structure, still in a perfect condition. This 50m high tower in Mandu was seven storeyed and built in red sandstone. Perhaps it paid the price for its hastily-built construction. It crumbled too soon. This is Mandu's most pathetic section of ruins.

The tomb of Hoshang Shah, completed about 1440, is remarkable for its elegant proportions combining grace and strength. It is a large cubical structure, with its four walls rising to 9.6m. A row of ornamental elephant tusk brackets support a projecting eave over which the parapet is carved with miniature arches. The main arch entrance on the southern side is flanked by two perforated screens also set within arched frames.

The tomb interior is square, 14.9m by 14.9m. It looks quite solemn. The exterior of the tomb is flat and heavy. The four corner turrets have a conical shape, placed rather too close to the central dome which is crowned with a crescent. Both internally and externally Hoshang Shah's tomb is reveted with white marble, the first of its kind before the Mughals started building palaces and tombs in marble in the seventeenth century.

To the west of this marble tomb stands a colonnade with three rows of pillars obtained from ruins of earlier structures.

The southern end of Mandu is occupied by numerous small tombs without any particular distinction-Malik Mugith's Masjid, Dai Ka Mahal, Darya Khan's tomb, Chappan Mahal etc. However, the palace of Baz Bahadur built around a stately lotus pool surrounded by graceful corridors and pavilions on the terrace, is a charming royal residence. There is an inscription in Persian which ascribes this building to Sultan Nasir Khan (1508-9). Perhaps, Baz Bahadur had it suitably altered for use as a pleasure place for his beloved Rupmati. It is a grand structure without any unnecessary ornament. The Rupmati pavilion is a rather austere structure, uninspiring in its battered walls and rugged appearance, built as a defence outwork soon after the Ghuris moved to Mandu from Dhar. The two pavilions on the uppermost terrace are the most charming portions, affording fabulous views of the Narmada meandering its leisurely course in the green valley lying hundreds of metres below. Baz Bahadur was a great lover of beauty and music but a miserable soldier. In 1561 he was comprehensively beaten by the Mughal armies led by Adham Khan at Sarangpur. He fled for life deserting Rupmati who poisoned herself rather than face humiliation.

The Nilkanth pavilion, built as a pleasure resort for Akbar, is reached after a descent of sixty steps. The central portion of the court has rooms to its east, west and south. The northern side is open for viewing the spectacular natural scenery. An elegantly designed cistern at the centre of the court provides the central point for royal gatherings and entertainments. Here Akbar was presented with a bevy of Mandu beauties. Later in Delhi Akbar discovered that Adham Khan had retained two dancers fancied by the young emperor. The issue was hushed up as Akbar's wet nurse Maham Angha had the two dancers killed to save her son Adham Khan from Akbar's fury.

Besides Mandu and Dhar, the Malwa style of Islamic architecture appeared at Chanderi, near Gwalior, which was also under the Ghuris and Khiljis of Mandu. The main features of architecture as seen at Mandu are manifest here as well but a few buildings show a definite strain of originality. The Kushk Mahal at Fathabad, originally a seven storeyed palace, was built by Mahmud Shah I in 1445 on his way back from Jaunpur. The upper three floors have caved down yet lower four surviving storeys provide enough evidence of the desire to experiment with new architectural designs. The plan of the Kushk Mahal is square with a diameter of 33m. There are halls at the four corners, with an entrance on each side. The most distinctive feature of the structure is the creation of two arched passages crossing at right angles, dividing the space between halls into four sections. The arches with a strong Ogee curve have a certain elegance.

The Jami Masjid has triple domes over the sanctuary and an impressive arched facade. The convoluted brackets are the chief ornamental features perhaps introduced by craftsman from Gujarat but these brackets were to be used more prominently in Akbar's buildings at Sikri and the Agra Fort.

Chanderi has only two tombs-Madarsa and Shahzadi ka Rauza but without any distinction of style or ornamentation. It is, however, the Badal Mahal Gateway, c1460, an independent architectural creation of some splendour, which deserves praise for the boldness of concept. The two tapering buttresses, typical of the Tughlaq buildings, contain the tall arch, decorated with spear-head fringes at the top. The elegance of jali screens on the upper portion of the arch has a delicate, fragile beauty. The surface ornamentation is of a high order. This triumphal arch is only an isolated example of genuine creative urge inspiring craftsmen to break away from the routine architectural style imitating the Tughlaqs at the Imperial capital.

facing page. Tomb of Hoshang Shah, Mandu.

right. Asharfi Mahal, opposite the Jama Masjid, Mandu.

9

GULBARGA,
BIDAR & DAULATABAD
THE BAHMANIS

The architecture of Gulbarga belongs to the earliest phase of Muslim rule in the southern part of India. In 1327 Muhammad Tughlaq shifted his capital to Daulatabad, carrying with him masons and artisans, scholars and sufis, merchants and labour. Gulbarga was a part of the Tughlaq rule but within twenty years Alauddin Bahman Shah claimed full independence in1347 to found here his own kingdom. The Bahmanis were known defenders of the Faith and were the first power in the subcontinent to exchange ambassadors with the Ottomans, recruited skilled personnel among Turks, Persians and Arabs. These foreigners were to form the most influential coterie of Afaqis, perennially in conflict with the Dakhinis or the local Sunni population including the Abyssinians.

Alauddin Bahman Shah (1347-1358) built a strong fort at Gulbarga, nearly three kilometres in circumference with semi circular bastions and gigantic battlements, protected by a 30m wide moat. The fort served as a nucleus of the growing Muslim power. The fort is an excellent example of defence architecture much inspired by similar works in Syria.

Jami Masjid (1367) built within the fort, has the rare distinction of being the only fully covered mosque in the country. It was designed by Rafi, a Persian architect. It covers a rectangular space of 66m by 52m. The three sides on the east, north and south provide space for wide cloisters. The whole interior contains rows of aisles forming 68 bays, each roofed by a cupola. The bays differ in size and the plain domes are

supported on faceted pendentives and starkly plain piers. The stilted spherical central dome rise over a substantial square clerestory letting in light and air. The most distinctive architectural feature of the Jami Masjid is the range of unusually wide archways raised over unusually low imposts.

The exterior of the mosque consists of arcaded openings. The northern side has an arched entrance, a later day addition. The fully covered interior of the Jami Masjid is a bold intellectual concept in mosque architecture but, excepting the two partially covered Tuglaq mosques in Delhi-the Kali Masjid (1370) and the Khirki Masjid (1375), this style remained unabsorbed in the indo-Islamic architectural tradition. The use of transverse vaulting parallels its use in such fourteenth century Iranian buildings as the congregational mosque at Abarquh but the low imposts and distinctive profile of the arches are quite different, owing considerable inspiration to the Persian origin of the patron and the architect.

Bala Hisar, a massive rectangular structure with semi-circular turrets, in an enigmatic building with no entrance save a narrow flight of steps to the top platform which has only some basic structures. It was, perhaps, the last resort under gravest circumstances. Most of the buildings within the fort have been destroyed or have collapsed. However, a market street leading to the western gate of the fort can still be identified for its rows of arched chambers under pyramidal vaults entered through an arched doorway, comparable to the famous Bazar Street for diamond merchants at Vijaynagar.

Outside the fort stands the Shah Bazar Mosque, the first mosque built in Gulbarga during the reign of Muhammad I (1358-75). The ground plan, including the sanctuary, is almost a square and contains a domed chamber on the eastern wall, an arched entrance on the north and south sides, a parapet of merlons with corner fluted finials and a flattish dome. The hall contains fifteen by six domed bays with no cloisters around the courtyard.

The tombs of the early Bahmani rulers stand on the western side of the fort. The tombs of Alauddin Bahman Shah (1358) and Muhammad I (1375) set the tone of architectural style for tombs built subsequently simple square domed chambers with slightly battered exterior, low, flattish domes and corner finials. The arch is angular and the whole structure is stark without any surface decoration.

Jami Masjid, Gulbarga.

Haft Gumbad or Seven Domes is a cluster of tombs belonging to the Gulbarga rulers. The tomb of Sultan Dawud (1378) is particularly noteworthy for its architectural experiment in creating two domed chambers linked by an interior narrow corridor. This double tomb is the first of its kind in the country. The tomb of Tajuddin Firoz (1422) shows a more advanced approach in terms of scale and decoration. It has two hemispherical domes, with a parapet of trefoil merlons and fluted corner finials over perpendicular walls, no longer battered in the Tughlaq mould. The

in much the same way as the popularity of the Saint Hazrat Nizamuddin clashed with the might and arrogance of Ghiyasuddin, the first Tughlaq sultan whose new fortress city of Tughlaqabad soon lay abandoned and deserted as cursed by the saint. Firoz wanted his dissolute son to be blessed by Hazrat Gesu Daraz. This denied, he had the saint move away to the outskirts of the Bahmani capital. After the death of Firoz in 1422 his brother Shihabuddin Ahmad I ascended the throne but Gulbarga lost its status as the Bahmani capital in favour of Bidar, and never quite

facade is divided both horizontally and vertically into arched recesses in two or three planes. The upper niches are covered with jali screens, angled eaves on brackets, decorative lotus, arabesque and roundels of geometrical designs-all executed on stucco. The interiors of these tombs are richly decorated with panels, bands, roundels and medallions.

Gulbarga, centuries after its creation, is still famous for the *dargah* of Hazrat Gesu Daraz, the renowned Chisti saint, who migrated to Gulbarga in his old age and settled in a monastery close to the Jami Masjid in the fort. The growing influence and popularity of the saint soon came into conflict with the ruler Firoz

regained its status and splendour, hereafter consigned to history as a deserted capital.

The tomb of Hazrat Gesu Daraz is an unpretentious square domed structure with a double storeyed facade containing nine sunken arches above and flanking the central arch, with sparse decoration. Also at the tomb complex is a later day mosque in the Bijapur style with its cluster of finials and dome raised over a bed of petals, and elegant brackets. The most outstanding architectural attraction at the dargah is an immense arch springing from two high towers pierced with arched window openings.

The dargah of Shah Kama Majarrad near the *dargah* of

previous page. Interior, Jami Masjid, Gulbarga

left. Entrance to the Dargah of Banda Nawaz, Gulbarga.

below. Layout plan of the Gulbarga Jami Masjid.

bottom. Gumbad Darwaza at the Bidar Fort.

Hazrat Gesu Daraz, is noteworthy for its splendid decoration in stucco-multi-lobed arches, bands and roundels, proliferating geometric and foliate designs etc. The pointed vault ceilings at the Langar ki Masjid imitates ribbings as on timber ceilings, a feature borrowed from the indigenous building style. The *dargah* of Sheikh Sirajuddin Junaidi, preceptor of the early Bahmani rulers is framed within two high minarets. The Chor Gumbad, built for Hazrat Gesu Daraz in 1420, was never used by the saint. The high dome, arched openings on the facade and miniature corner towers lend it a distinctive appearance.

BIDAR

Bidar was already a part of the Bahmani kingdom when the capital was moved here from Gulbarga in 1425. The pressure caused by dissensions between the Afaqi nobles and the Dakhinis, close proximity of the Gulbarga border with their perennial enemy state of Vijaynagar, coupled with the widening rift and tension accruing from increasing hold of Shia Islam were among the prominent compelling reasons for this move. Besides, Bidar had a better climate and natural resources to justify the choice. The Persian influence, however, continued unabated to affect the architectural style at Bidar.

The mosques in Bidar show a marked preference for the classic and chaste simplicity of architectural style. Solah Khamba Mosque, built in 1327 during the rule of Muhammad Tughlaq, is the earliest mosque here. The long prayer hall is divided into nineteen by five domed bays. The columns are circular and

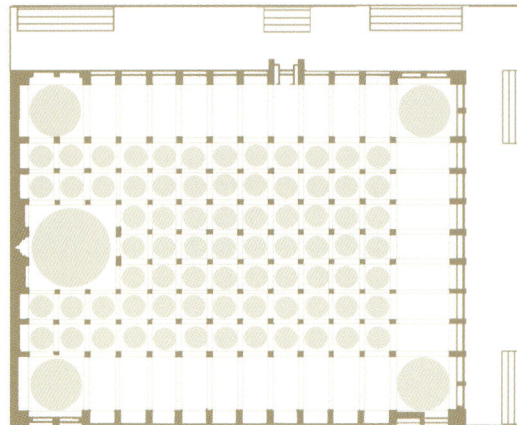

massive. The mihrab is framed by a multi-lobed arch. The unadorned surface of the mosque has its own unique elegance.

Takht mahal, the royal palace of Shihabuddin Ahamd I is now in utter ruins, only the western gateway retains some of its original tile work and the royal emblems of the tiger and the sun. Carved stone bases of the columns in timber have survived in the large Diwan-i-Aam. The best preserved structure is the Rangin Mahal, mostly remodeled for Ali Barid. The wooden structure finds much use for carved brackets and beams inlaid with mother-of-pearl. Traces of original decoration in plaster are also seen at Takht-i-Kirmani.

The Jami Masjid at Bidar is an elegant structure with seven arched openings on the front. The piers in the interior are plain. The Baridis did much restoration work on this mosque.

The Madarsa built in by Mahmud Gawan, the famous minister of Muhammad III, in 1472 is perhaps the most outstanding building in Bidar. In both concept and execution of detail, the Madarsa is "a piece of Persia in India", as Percy Brown calls it. In fact, Mahmud Gawan, a sophisticated Persian merchant settled at Bidar, emerged as the *de facto* ruler of Bidar between 1461 and 1481. He maintained the delicate balance between the Afaqis and Dakhinis by giving high offices to both the parties. But the Dakhinis held a permanent unhealing grudge against the influential Persian. They forged a treasonable letter with his seal. The ruler gave his minister a summary trial without enquiring about the truth. Gawan was beheaded in 1481. When the truth opened the eyes of Muhammad III, he tore his hair under fits of remorse. Strangely enough, the king is long since forgotten but Mahmud Gawan's memory has survived for the magnificent school he built in Bidar.

The structure of the Madarsa, in three storeys, is built around a courtyard, four arcaded portals surmounted by fully bulbous domes on high domes. The eastern facade had two tall domed minarets. Only one of these minarets has survived destruction. Every detail of work at the Madarsa speaks of an unmistakable Persian character.

The whole exterior of the Madarsa is covered with glazed tiles in glowing hues-green yellow and white. Precautions were taken against possible seepage damaging the glaze of the tiles by inserting sheets of lead between masonry courses. The Madarsa is still amongst the most magnificent buildings in the provincial capitals despite a slightly over-emphasized display of applied art for its own sake, "a testament to the pervasive influence of the Persian Afaqis at the Bahmani court", as underlined by George Michell.

If glorious tilework and Persianised design has earned the madarsa some admiration, it is also the cause of much disenchantment amongst critics like Sir Wolsley Haig who find that "there is little or no feeling in Mahmud Gawan's college for plastic form and mass, or for the values of contrasted light and shade. The architect has visualised his subject as the architects of Eastern Persia habitually did in two rather than in three dimensions. For sheer loveliness of colour the result could hardly be better; but divest the building of its superficial ornament and little is left save a mathematically correct, tame and highly stylized fabric". For sure, there is little effort here to adapt this Persian model to its present environment. The madarsa is surely an outstanding architectural creation but it relates to nothing in Bidar: it does not belong here.

The tombs at Ashtur, the royal neoropolis show the general

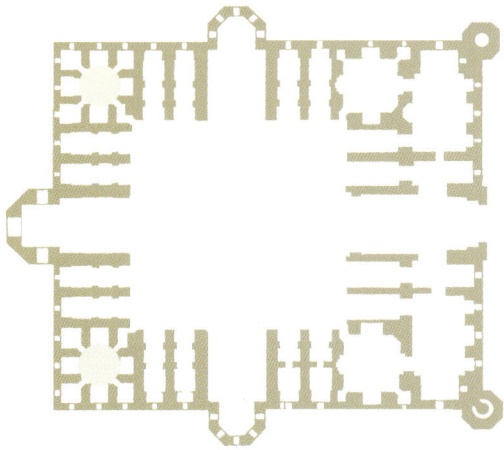

top left. The Madarsa of Khwaja Mahmud Gawan, Bidar.

top right. Decortion with Persian tiles on the minar at the Madarsa, Bidar.

above. Layout plan of the Madarsa, Bidar.

right. Tomb of Mahmud, Bidar.

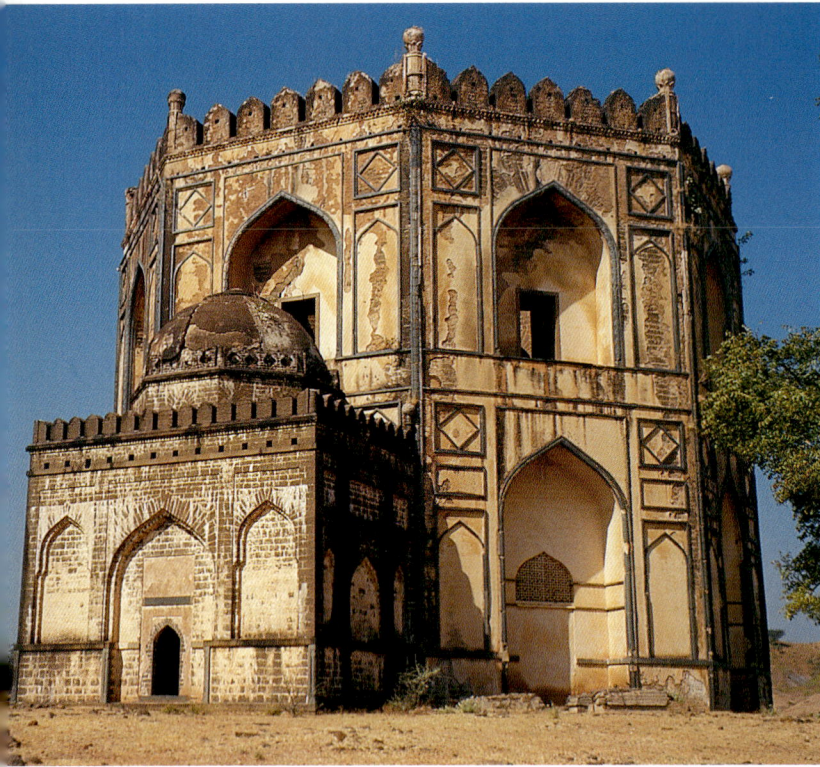

left. Tomb of Khalil Allah, (Chaukhandi), Bidar.

below. Jami Masjid, Daulatabad.

acceptance of the bulbous Tartar dome over straight-walled cubical structures, a sophisticated and advanced architectural element. The tomb of Shihabuddin Ahmad (1436) is a grand structure with three tiers of pointed recessed arches on the façade, seven on the uppermost and four on each of the middle and lower panels. The parapet of merlons with corner finials adds majestic grandeur to the structure. These merlons are repeated over the sixteen sided drum of the dome. The interior contains specimens of exquisite Persian decoration-bands ad panels in brilliant gold, vermilion, green and turquoise colours.

The tomb of Alauddin Ahmad II (1458) has five differently sized arched recesses in gentle double curves on the facade. The central arch is the largest. The exterior has square panels above the arched recesses. Chawkhandi-a square domed chamber encased within a double-storeyed octagon, is the tomb of the Shia saint Khalil Allah (1460). The tomb of Mahmud (1518) also uses triple tiers of arched recesses on the façade.

The later Baridi rulers chose to be buried to the west of the town. The tomb style shows certain signs of evolution in the use of four-centred arched recesses and openings with the central arch being the widest, elaboration of the parapet and foliate bands around fully formed bulbous domes. The most impressive tomb here belongs to Ali Barid Shah (1580). The high stilted domed chamber is open on all the four sides. Traces of some exquisite tilework on bands and panels in the interior evidence

taste for refined decoration. The dome is supported on pendentives forming a net-like pattern, and arabesques in stucco. The other tombs show little innovation in architectural style, only repeating the best features on earlier tombs.

DAULATABAD

Daulatabad, north-west of Gulbarga, was already a renowned fort during the rule of Muhammad Tughlaq who occupied it in 1327. The fortifications girdling the awesome conical hill look impregnable with its extremely precipitous scarp, concentric battlemented walls and tunneled passages, heated chambers virtually deathtraps for the enemy. The Daulatabad Fort was the greatest fort in the whole of southern India, an example of the most amazing defence network known to the medieval world, mostly the work of Yadavas. Muhammad Tughlaq changed its name from Devanagiri to Daulatabad. The Bahmanis, surrounded on all sides by enemies like Vijaynagar, Warangal and Orissa, were obliged to strengthen its defence in vigilance against any invasion. In fact, the Daulatabad fort has remained invincible, unconquered by any enemy.

The great conical hill, 200m high, commands a magnificent site. It stands detached from the spurs of the Sahyadri range. Its lower portion is scarped upto 65m from the ground level, presenting a vertical unassailable face-work of the Yadava rulers.

The Daulatabad Fort contains few structures of any significant architectural merit, except the Mughal pavilion which was Shahjahan's favourite resort here. Further up at the acropolis is a large platform with gun mountings and guns stationed in a defence line-up. The only two structures of some interest are the Jami Masjid and the Chini Mahal, built by Qutbuddin Mubarak Khilji in 1318. The mosque uses 106 pillars from temples. The workmanship is rather crude. Chini Mahal is actually a portion of a splendid gateway built by the later Nizam Shai rulers.

The only structure of architectural merit is the Chand Minar, built in 1435 during the rule of Alauddin Ahmad II (1436-58). It is a remarkable tower, 30m high and four storeyed, built nearly forty years before the m adarsa in Bidar. The three circular galleries are supported by carved brackets. The surface is very discreetly decorated with string courses, blind merlons, vertical flutings and blind arches. The circular form of the minar is slightly tapering toward the crest. Again, this minar also shows that the architects were inspired by similar towers in Persia which remained the fountain-head of inspiration for all ambitious architectural undertakings during the Bahmani rule.

The forts at Raichur, Narnala, Naldurg and Parenda were all great defence citadels with elaborate arrangements for security. Clearly those who built these forts were well acquainted with the structures of defence forts in the west and the engineering skill with which provisions for defence against surprise attacks was provided through tunnels, traverses and redoubts.

left. Chand Minar at the Daulatabad Fort.

10

GOLCONDA & HYDERABAD
THE QUTB SHAHIS

The breakdown of the Bahamani kingdom in 1489 led to the creation of five fiercely ambitious states (Ahmadnagar, Bijapur, Golconda, Bidar and Berar). Quli Qutbul Mulk, a high official at Bidar of Turkman origin at Bidar, inherited Golconda which had been under the Kakatiyas of Warangal. The Bahamanis at Gulbarga strengthened Mangalawaram or Mankal the original mud fort at Golconda. However, it was only after the founding of the Qutb Shahi kingdom by Quli Qutbul Mulk in 1489 that this boulder-strewn, 123m high hill was covered with strong fortifications, rising and descending with the contours of the hill.

The Golconda fort is an illustrious example of defence architecture, an irregular rhombus with a rough pentagon (known as the new fort or Naya Qila) added to its north-eastern side in 1624. The hill is surrounded by a meandering crenellated granite wall nearly 2.5km in circumference with 87 semi-circular bastions, eight gateways and four drawbridges, further secured by a deep moat running below the towering ramparts. Huge cannons still stand mounted on strategically important bastions. Later day successors of Qutbul Mulk added grand palaces to the fort. The most important portions of Golconda was destroyed by Aurangzeb in 1686 when the eight-month long siege of the fort by the Mughal armies finally finished the Qutb Shahi rule.

The Fateh Darwza admits visitors to the walled citadel. It is magnificent and strong, made of heavy teak and studded with sharp iron spikes to thwart elephants crashing against it. Built of solid granite this massive gateway is 15m high. There is a small window just above the entrance through which hot oil could be poured over intruders forcing entry, a typical medieval defence strategy. Further on stand Habshi Kamans, two splendid square arched portals which housed the ruler's Abyssinian guards. The Jami Masjid to the right of these arches was built in 1518 by Sultan Quli Qutbul Mulk, earliest specimen of the Qutb Shahi architecture. It is a robust structure built within an enclosed area. The sanctuary has a four-arched façade. Broad and pointed arches still appear grand. The central mihrab is carved with a chain motif. The stone steps and narrow pathways connect one huge boulder to another huge boulder, the gap sometimes filled with brick and mud to create negotiable tracks. Along these paths clay pipes fitted into the wall flanks, evidence of the splendid water supply arrangement for the upper terraces. A series of Persian wheels carried water from the reservoirs to upper terraces from where the pipes channelised it into baths, gardens, cisterns and kitchens. This is a sixteenth century engineering marvel.

The mosque built by Ibrahim Qutb Shah stands near the crest of the fort. It is distinguished by its prominent corner minarets. The small courtyard extends upto the ramparts. The Balahisar Baradari, 130m above ground level, and 380 steps away from the Grand Portico, is a triple storeyed structure with twelve arches built on substantial piers. A raised chamber with triple arches opens off the rear wall affording picturesque view of the landscape below. A stone throne stands on the open terrace. The *Baradari* served as an audience hall and also as a pleasure pavilion.

The Rani Mahal zenana quarters are built on massive platforms. These palaces, now in complete ruins, have massive arches, vaulted chambers, Turkish baths, and rows upon rows of decorative niches and cornices. There are traces of splendid plaster decoration- delicate arabesques in the roundels. The Rani Mahal was subjected to vindictive destruction by the Mughal forces. Near the portico at the Blahisar Darwaza stands a double-storeyed pavilion, office of Akanna and Madanna, ministers of Abdullas Qutb Shah. Ruins of Nagina Bagh, a walled garden, can still be observed near the portico. The number of unidentifiable structures standing in sheer heaps of stones is too large to be overlooked but remains a frustrating exercise in investigation. The tombs of the Qutb Shahi rulers stand in a cluster beyond the Banjara Gate of the fort. These seven tombs are similar in architectral style.

The tomb of Quli Jamshed is an octagonal, double-storeyed structure. Its style is noteworthy for the use of elaborate brackets supporting projected balconies at two levels and a matching crenellated cornice with small minarets at each angle. The hemispherical dome is a little too ponderous for this small structure which has no added plinth to create the advantage of height.

Muhammad Quli's tomb stands on a double terrace. The facade is in the pillar and lintel style. The columns are 6.6m in height. The tomb is covered with exhuberant ornamentation - floral and geometrical motif especially on the cornice. The tomb structure is unique in its use of timber columns framing the entrance portals in the middle of each side. The corner minarets also carry the usual decorative elements but are built in a miniature form. The dome rises over an elevated square terrace which is internally octagonal.

The tomb of Ibrahim Qutb Shah stands on a high plinth. There are seven arches on each side of the square ground floor and five blind arches on each side of the upper terrace. The tomb of Hayat Baksh Begum, only child of Muhammad Quli, is a

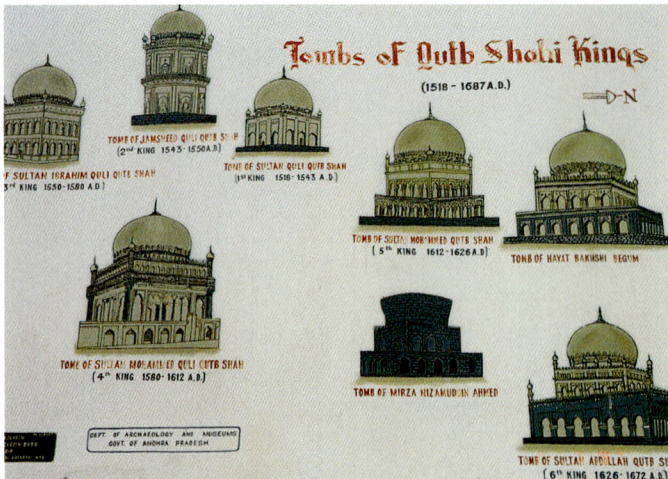

lovely structure to which a mosque was added by Aurangzeb. It is double-storeyed, standing on a terrace which is surmounted by a large dome with a pinnacle of 30.5m. There are six arches on the ground and five arches on the upper storey.

The largest tomb in Ibrahim Bagh belongs to Adullah Qutb Shah, the sixth ruler. It has a seven arched facade on the ground floor and five-arched façade on the upper floor, surrounded by a hanging balcony, merlons and numerous finials. Traces of glazed tile decoration and elegant stucco work are still to be seen. The earliest tomb here belongs to Quli Qutbul Mulk. It shows its Bahamani derivation in its simple outline and sparse decoration. The outer walls of the tomb are divided into triple-arched panels on each face. The tomb has an octagonal interior.

The architectural style of the Qutb Shahi tombs has a uniform, though distinctive character. "They are", as George Michell observes, "typically square buildings with arcaded storeys, supported on massive plinths which may also be arcaded. The lower storeys are surmounted by crenellated parapets with small bulbous minarets protruding at each corner. Rising above the middle of the structure is a tall drum, which may be arcaded and balustraded. This supports a single dome, slightly bulbous in contour, rising from a frieze of petals or trefoil merlon motifs. The granite building material is usually covered with stucco and with coloured tilework. The projecting cornices are covered with plaster designs; this, and the addition of miniature arcaded galleries encircling the corner minarets, are characteristic features of the Qutb Shahi style".

The Qutb Shahi tombs suffer from an inordinate proclivity towards "an increased use of involuted moulded patterns". The ornamentation on stucco is, according to Percy Brown, "of a meretricious kind, enfeebling the outlines of the building and confusing its surfaces. …fanciful pinnacles and flimsy battlements with other purposeless embellishment of like a nature". It is however, in the design of the ceiling where the Qutb Shahi architect displays his ingenuity. "In the interior, owing to the size and especially the increased height of the dome

it was found necessary to cover the mortuary chamber at a suitable height with a curved ceiling, leaving the interior of the dome above as a great unused void, a structural system not exactly of double doming as was now being practised in northern India by the Mughals, but an expedient with much the same object in view".

The splendour of the Qutb Shahi architecture is not so much represented by the ruins at Golconda fort or the tombs of rulers as it is by the great triumphal arch-the Charminar (1594) at the centre of Hyderabad which displays strength, elegance, and a remarkable inventiveness in concept and the execution of details. Hyderabad, first known as Bhagnagar, was founded in 1592 by Muhammad Quli Shah. The French traveller Tavernier in 1653 compared Hyderabad to Orleans, "well built and opened out". In 1672 Abbe Carr was much impressed by Hyderabad "as the centre of all trade in the East".

Charminar has four wide roads radiating in the four cardinal directions. The four minarets, from which this monumental structure derives its name, command the city centre. It is a square structure, each side measuring 100 feet with a high pointed arch at the centre on each side. The whole structure contains numerous small decorative arches arranged both vertically and horizontally. The prominently projected cornice over the first floor upholds a series of six arches and capitals on each facade, rising to the second storey of the minarets. The projected canopy, ornamental brackets and decoration in stucco plaster add to the beauty of the two upper storeys beginning with a substantial arcaded triforium over which rises a smaller arcade and a perforated balustrade. The uppermost terrace was also used as a school and for prayers at the small mosque.

The minarets, their domed finials, rise to 180 feet from the ground. An interesting seventeenth century description of this monument comes from Thevenot: "That which is called the four towers, is a square building, of which each face is ten fathom broad and about seven high. It is opened on the four sides by four arches. There are two galleries in it, one over another, and

facing page, left. Plan of the tombs at Golconda Fort.

facing page, right. Fountain within the palace ruins, Golconda Fort.

right. Tile decoration on a tomb at Golconda.

below. Tomb of Muhammad Ali Qutb Shah, founder of Hyderabad.

all over a terrace that serves for a roof, bordered with a stone balcony; and at each corner of the building a tower about ten fathom high and each tower has four galleries with little arches on the outside… It is vaulted underneath and appears like a dome."

Near the Charminar stand four magnificent arches called Char Kaman facing the four cardinal points which once marked entrance to the royal places. These are called Machli Kaman, Kali Kaman, Sher Gill Ki Maman and Charminar ki Kaman. The Char-su-ka-Hauz, a cistern with a fountain in the centre of these arches is now called Gulzar Hauz. Nearly all the palaces have disappeared. Still, the mosques in Hyderabad have survived.

Work on the Mecca Masjid, near the Charminar, was started by Muhammad Qutb Shah in 1617 and completed by Aurangzeb in 1693. It is a grand edifice with a spectacular courtyard, large

enough to accommodate ten thousand men at prayer. The sanctuary consists of five by three enlarged bays, domed except for the central bay which has a pointed vault. The minarets appear rather stunted despite their arcaded balconies and domed finials. Mecca Masjid is 225 feet long, 108 feet wide, and 75 feet high. A particular stone brick in the mihrab is believed to have been made of sacred earth brought from Mecca. The whole structure seems to rise over mammoth boulders and gigantic stones painstakingly rolled over to the site from the hills surrounding the city.

The small Jami Masjid, near the Charminar, was built by Muhammad Quli Qutb Shah in 1592. It is, however, the Toli Masjid which is one of the finest specimens of the Qutb Shahi architecture. The sanctuary has two compartments with the outer having five and the inner having three archways. Niches built in the pillar and lintel style replace the two arches from the outer front. The minarets, topped by domed finials, are divided into two arcaded storeys above the parapet level by galleries supported by elegant brackets and rich mouldings. The parapet is rather high and formed by row of perforated arch-screens crowned by merlons and small domical turrets. The cut-plaster decoration at the Toli Masjid is the chief source of its beauty.

Besides the Charminar, Mecca Masjid and the Toli Masjid in Hyderabad, there are two other contemporary buildings which evidence the concern for strength and elegance typical of the Qutb Shahi architecture. Both Dar-ush-Shifa (a hospital and caravan serai) and the Badshahi Ashurkhana (congregation hall where Shia Muslims gather during Muharram to mourn the martyrdom of Hazrat Imam Husain in the battle of Karbala) were built in 1595 and 1596 respectively by Muhammad Quli Qutb Shah as part of an elaborate architectural scheme for his new capital.

facing page. Minarets of the Toli Masjid, Hyderabad.

above. Upper portion of Char Minar, Hyderabad.

below. Golconda Fort.

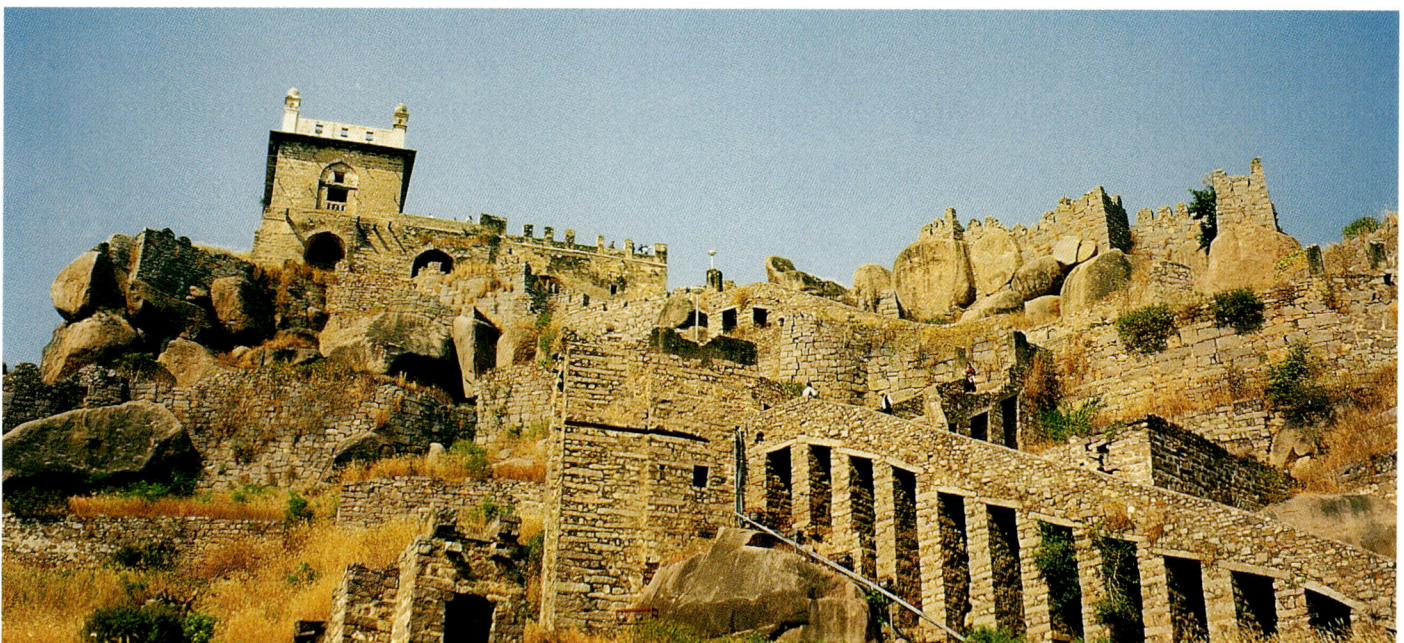

11
BIJAPUR
THE ADIL SHAHIS

Bijapur was a city of considerable political importance even before it was captured by Alauddin Khilji in 1294. The Muslim population kept growing as testified by the building of Karimuddin's Mosque in 1320. When Bijapur became part of the Gulbarga sector of the Bahamani rule, the city grew still more important. Bijapur became the capital of the new Adil Shahi rulers following the debacle of Bidar in 1481. It was Yusuf Adil Khan of Turkish origin and on officer of the Bahamani chief Khwaja Mahmud Gawan who established his own small kingdom in Bijapur in 1490. Yusuf ruled for nearly twenty years till his death in 1510. His succcessors-Ismail (1510-1534), Ibrahim I (1535-1558), Ali I (1558-1580), Ibrahim II (1580-1627), Mohammad (1627-1656) and Ali II (1656-1672) were all able rulers, each inspired with a vision to make Bijapur the most splendid capital in southern India. They made their own contributions to the immense architectural heritage of Bijapur. Even in its present ruinous state Bijapur has a great number of mosques tombs and palaces in a fair state of preservation. The main citadel and the city wall, work of Yusuf and Ali I, was completed by 1565.

Ibrahim Roza and the Mosque, Bijapur.

With each new ruler trying to surpass in beauty and splendour, the work of his predecessor, Bijapur continued to receive additions to its list of impressive buildings, reaching its zenith during the first half of the seventeenth century. The Adil shahis virtually competed with the grand Mughals in the creation of aesthetically satisfying architecture. Bijapur architecture, however, suffered a little in comparison to the Mughal buildings for want of white marble. The great buildings in Bijapur are still remarkable for their grand concept and execution, the most aesthetically and constructionally competent manifestation of architecture in the whole of the Deccan.

The Old Jami Masjid, built in 1513, soon after Yusuf's death, is the first building of the Adil Shahi rule. It shows no trace of any tentative effort, instead it shows that the architects had already acquired full knowledge of their craft and mastered the art and science of architecture. This mosque has a single hemispherical dome rising above a ring of petals. The prayer chamber has three bays, the central bay being the widest. Other mosques like Ikhlas Khan's mosque and Ibrahim's Old Jami Mosque are noteworthy for emphasizing vertical projections above the roof with turrets divided into several horizontal courses by plasterwork. The cornices and the brackets supporting these projections are quite prominent. The roofs are mostly flat, not domed or vaulted. The round medalion supported on voluted brackets, chief ornamental motif used on

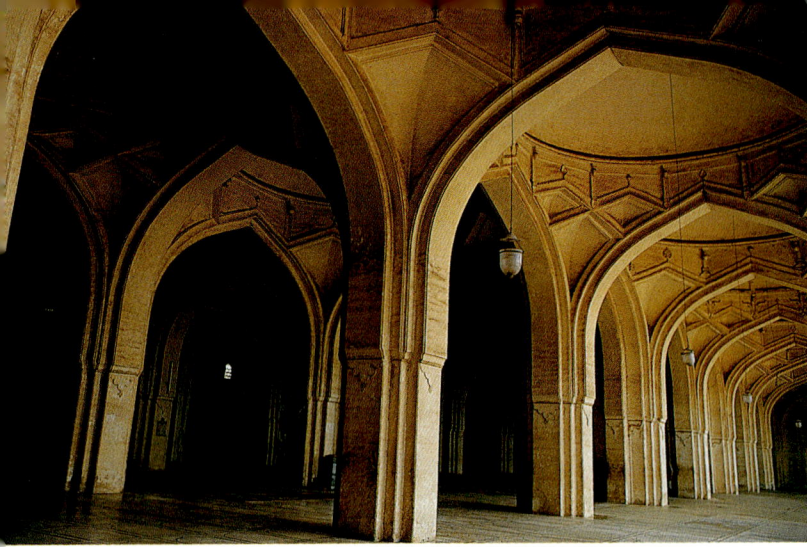

the spandrel of the arches, makes its first appearance at Ikhlas Khan's Mosque. These architectural features were to become recognisable characteristics of the Adil Shahi style. The spherical shape of the dome rising like a well-formed bud out of a ring of petals, ornamental turrets on the parapet, four-centred arches with a fuller curve raised on heavy and massive piers with rectangular sections, and almost a complete absence of pillars in buildings, sparse decoration on stucco-are some of the striking features of the Adil Shahi architecture.

The Jami Masjid, the great congregational mosque of the capital, is one of the finest mosques in India. It is a sober and massive structure, built between 1557 and 1686, most of it during the reign of Adil Shah I who acquired enormous wealth after the sack of Vijaynagar in 1565. The area of the courtyard is nearly 91,000 square feet. With the later extension of its length towards the east, the total comes to nearly 116,000 square feet. The Jami Masjid is remarkable for its harmonious proportions and dignified simplicity. The grand prayer hall is divided into forty five compartments. The nave in the centre is a square area of seventy six feet, with twelve arches, three on each side. These intersecting arches create an octagonal cornice on which rises the base of the dome. The mihrab, behind the curtain, has some elegant ornamentation.

The single hemispherical dome is massive and extremely impressive. An arcaded fenestration around the sides of the clerestory, notable merlons over the parapet and a string of petals girdling the base of the dome-all contribute to a dignified and splendid upper structure. The metal finial is crowned by a crescent, Aurangzeb's contribution to the Jami Masjid is limited to extension of the courtyard and building of corridors on the southern and the northern side, and a gateway on the eastern wall. The exterior on the northern wall has a facade of double-storeyed arcades. The Jami Masjid has no high corner towers.

Gagan Mahal, built by Adil Shah I (1561) is an impressive palace-cum-audience hall with three magnificent arch entrances. The central arch is the widest and tallest arch of its kind, nearly sixty feet wide and fifty feet in height. The first floor, meant for the Zenana, has now completely collapsed, only the twelve alcoves in the walls indicate its former grandeur. Much of the wooden construction, including four massive columns supporting the upper floor, has been destroyed. The medalion-and-bracket

appears in full glory at the expansive spandrels at Gagan Mahal. The bracket depicts a fish head down, supporting the medalion on the flukes of the tail. This is the ornamental version of the Mahi Maratib, the fish banner, still in use on Muharram in this Shia state. Gagan Mahal, despite its present ruinous condition, gives enough evidence of its original splendour. The sheer dimension of its grand arches shows the importance of this hall in the architectural scheme within the citadel of the Adil Shahis.

Close to Gagan Mahal is a seven-storeyed tower, once a palace or a watch tower overlooking the moat girdling the ramparts on the citadel wall. Under its shadow stands a small structure-Jal Mahal, set within a tank. It was part of the recreational garden meant for the royalty.

The Ibrahim Rauza is amongst the most beautiful buildings of the Adil Shahis. Originally meant to receive the mortal remains of Taj Sultana, the queen, it came to be used as the tomb of Ibrahim II who pre-deceased the queen in 1627. The rauza has the most remarkable proportions, exquisite minarets, cupolas, parapets and brackets. It is built on a high plinth which it shares with the mosque.

The central square chamber houses the various tombs. It is enclosed within a verandah of seven arches of unequal dimensions on each side. The two narrow arches on each face add a delicate artistic variety in the voids. The ceiling of the central chamber-eighteen feet square, is an example of ingeniously applied architectural expertise: the masonry is juggle-jointed with no visible external support. The Bijapur architects created a 'hanging ceiling' in evidence of their consummate skill. Surface decoration in the interior and the verandah has a amazing variety with crosses, lotuses and wheels. In fact, every inch of available surface has been covered with splendid geometrical and inscriptional carvings. The elaborately carved brackets and the battlemented upper storey supporting the dome are of extraordinary elegance. The three-quarter dome set upon a ring of petals looks striking in its sensuous contours. Open turrets topped with similarly fashioned miniature domes stand above the piers of the arches below. The base of the dome is hidden behind a square façade. Each corner has domed turret. The merlons on the parapet provide another feature of exterior ornamentation. The four corner minars are slender, their apex terminating well below the full height of the dome. The Ibrahim Rauza is a garden tomb built to perfection and its artistic excellence remains unequalled amongst buildings of its kind in southern India.

Close to the rauza lies the Taj Bawdi, built by Ibrahim II in memory of his queen. The giant archway flanked by two octagonaI towers provides a grand setting for the water reservoir which is still in good use, particularly during the hot summer months. At Jodi Gumbed (Twin Domes) are buried the two traitors-Khan Muhammad and Khawas Khan, father and son, who helped Aurangzeb defeat the last Adil Shahi ruler.

The Sherza bastion, between the Shahpur and Mecca gates, is one of the massive bastions on the city wall, now mostly destroyed. It still upholds the 4.45m long cannon Malik-i-Maidan, set up by Muhammad Adil Shah. Weighing 55 tons, it is believed to be one of the largest cannons in the world. The muzzle shows an elephant caught in the open mouth of a lion. A grand view of the city can be obtained from the top of the bastion.

Asar Mahal was built by Muhammad Adil Shah in 1591 to house the two scared hairs of the Prophet Muhammad. The palace has a grand five-arched facade and still remains one of the most elegant buildings in Bijapur. Mihtar Mahal, gateway to an unbuilt mosque, is an extremely ornate double-storeyed structure, particularly known for its exquisitely carved long brackets supporting the projecting balconies and trellis work. It belongs to the last years of Ibrahim II's reign.

The Gol Gumbed (1656) is the most stupendous creation of the Adil Shahi rulers. It is well known as the single largest dome in the whole world. This square structure is the tomb of Muhammad Adil Shah (1627-1656). The dome is 51m high with a diameter of 37m. The whole structure has been raised on walls with a thickness of three metres. The dome unsupported by any external pillar or contrivance is an engineering marvel. Basically the Gol Gumbad is a large cube. Each side of the cube has three shallow arches with the central and largest arch providing entrance to the tomb.

The massive dome structure has a simple dignified appearance. It has been accomplished in an astonishing manner. "The conversion of the square below into a circle above was achieved by ingeniously by arranging each arch "so that its feet stood within the sides of the square plan, but with its plane of surface at an angle, the intersection above producing the eight sided figure on which the circular cornice was projected. The interior surface of the dome is set back some twelve feet from the inner edge of this circle, so that a portion of its weight is transmitted directly downwards on to the four walls, the remainder being carried on the intersecting arches which also receive and counteract any outward thrust", observes renowned historian Percy Brown. The dome itself is constructed of horizontal courses of brick with a substantial layer of mortar between each course, in other words it consists of a homogeneous shell or monobloc of concrete reinforced with bricks, the whole being of an average thickness of ten feet. It is a marvellous architectural achievement particularly when no scaffolding or wooden centering was being used except, perhaps for the apex below the crown. The expertise for this structure was derived from Ottoman sources or from Persia. Like the Pantheon at Rome and St.Sophia at Istanbul, the Gol Gumbad at Bijapur is one of the largest single-domed structures in the world, a work of sheer phenomenal splendours.

The Gol Gumbad is enriched by all the familiar features of the Adil Shahi architecture: the wide projected cornices, brackets, petal ring surrounding the neck of the dome. The solitary note of

slight disharmony is caused by the seven-storeyed octagonal corner towers bearing a Chinese pagoda-like look but under the shadow of this magnificent architectural creation this appears but a minor incongruity. The Gol Gumbad is not an isolated structure: it stands as the central building in a massive architectural enterprise including a mosque, Naqqar Khana, guest houses-all enclosed within a walled garden.

But the most impressive structure in Bijapur is Bara Kaman, a mere structural skeleton of the uncompleted tomb of Ali Adil Shah II. Its twelve graceful arches testify to the grand building plans which, if realised, would have surpassed in beauty the memorials of his predecessors. Work on this structure was abandoned following the ruler's death in 1672.

The Adil Shahi architecture throughout retained a very high standard till its end in 1686 when Aurangzeb annexed Bijapur.

KHANDESH

Khandesh, situated between the Deccan and Gujarat, became an independent state in 1382, founded by Malik Raja Faruqi. The Faruqi kings ruled for nearly two hundred years, first from Thalner and later on from Burhanpur. The Khandesh architecture shows a mature form, no doubt influenced by the architecture of neighbouring states.

The tombs at Thalner form a definite group of buildings with a distinctive character and identity. The original inspiration for the square tomb came from Hoshang Shah's tomb at Mandu. The tomb of Miran Mubarak Faruqi (1441-1457) shows a certain attempt at introducing new features like wider spacing between doors and windows, parapet over the eaves and an increased height of the dome by using an octagonal drum and stilting of its sides. These features were combined well to create a pleasing architectural effect.

The Bibi ki Masjid at Burhanpur (c.1590) is a mosque of the closed variety with a large central arched entrance flanked by two minarets. The use of oriel window on the uppermost stage of the minars is a very distinctive structural innovation. The mosque, however is not known for any particular feature and merely uses a familiar, conventionalised form.

The Jami Masjid at Burhanpur (1589) is a large and impressive structure with a facade of fifteen pointed arches, set within two tall minarets at the corners. The mosque has excellent proportions and a general harmonious tone. The Jami Masjid at Asirgarh, the Idgah Khajuri mosques, and the Adil Shahi tombs are excellent examples of mosque and tomb architecture. The only structure of some distinction is the square tomb of Shah Nawaz Khan a Mughal governor. It incorporates structural features from Gujarat, Delhi and Bijapur. This tomb is the last building of any architectural significance in Khandesh.

facing page. Uper portion of the Gol Gumbad, Bijapur.

below. Gol Gumbad, Bijapur.

12

SHER SHAH

The course of architectural activity in northern India continued unaffected by the political turmoil caused by the annihilation of the Lodis and the founding of the Mughal empire by Babur in 1526. Babur chose to stay in Agra, the old Lodi capital, and Humayun, succeeding to the throne in 1530, also did not move to Delhi till the end of the next decade. The uncertainty surrounding the early years of Mugahal rule saw Sher Shah, an Afghan chief, rise to power in Bihar and pose a threat to the mild-mannered, astrologer, opium-lover second Mughal king. Sher Shah ultimately succeeded in throwing Humayun out of power in 1540 and forcing him to seek shelter and support in Persia. Sher Shah himself liked Bihar, the scene of his military exploits. He chose to build tombs for his family in Sasaram, a small provincial town in Bihar. These octagonal tombs carried forward the tradition of such tombs begun by Tilangani during 1368-69.

The tomb of Hasan Khan, father of Sher Shah (1535) is not much different from the tombs of Mubarak Sayyid and Muhammad Sayyid in Delhi. It is built within an enclosed area with all the trappings of a royal tomb though Hasan Khan was not a king. Sher Shah gave his father an octagonal tomb only to gain respectability for his humble origin and authority. The tomb has no plinth, a fact which deprives the huge structure of architectural dignity. The absence of battered piers at the angles

Tomb of Sher Shah at Sasaram, Bihar.   inset. Tomb of Hasan Shah Sur, Sasaram, Bihar.

the octagon gives the structure a vertical thrust towards the dome. The roof over the verandah is crowned with four small domes over each side of the octagon. The drum of the dome is a rather plain high wall without fenestrations creating an ungainly appearance. A hexagonal chhattri over each angle appears over this drum. The massive dome is crowned with a double lotus and triple kalasa finial. Surely, Aliwal Khan, Sher Shah's architect was experimenting with the size he had observed in Delhi without achieving much success in his first attempt at this tomb.

The tomb of Sher Shah, built during his lifetime, is the second octagonal tomb in Sasaram. Built in five stages, this majestic tomb seems to emerge out of the placid blue waters of the large artificial lake surrounding it - a clear allusion to the waters of paradise as described in the Quran. The paradise imagery associated with tomb architecture was to appear in full glory in the Mughal tombs.

The tomb stands on a terrace which forms the square courtyard with a pavilion at each corner and two oriel windows placed on each of the four sides. The lower storey comprises the cenotaph chamber enclosed by the octagonal verandah with three arches on each face of the eight sides, shaded by a chhajja over which rises the high crenellated parapet. There are chhattris at each angle of the octagonal structure. A second line of chhattris appears atop the drum encircling the massive dome crowned by a lotus finial. The Indian architects have created a splendid tomb in yellow Chunar sandstone, a noteworthy achievement for its excellent proportions, variety and distribution of its tonal values, breadth and scale of each major element and, finally, the carefully adjusted mass of the total conception.

The interior of the octagonal cenotaph hall is impressive, being 21.79m in diametre and 31.04m in height upto the soffit of the dome. The total height of the tomb is 37.57m. The octagonal structure posed few difficulties in the 'phase of transition' is the beam-and-bracket method, supplemented by an arched niche

below left. Lal Darwaza built by Sher Shah, opposite Purana Qila in Delhi.
below right. Interior of Jamali Kamali Mosque, Delhi.
facing page. Humayun Darwaza, Purana Qila, Delhi.

functioning as squinch at each angle. Light is admitted through jali windows on the drum and the overhanging oriel windows. Originally the tomb was decorated with glazed tiles in red, blue, yellow and white and the dome painted in white creating the effect of royal splendour.

The tomb was, as an afterthought, attached to the mainland by a causeway, approached through a domed gateway.

The tomb of Salim Shah (d.1552) was intended to be a still grander affair but, due to unpredictable change of fortunes, was left incompleted. Work could not proceed beyond the truncated core masonry, bases of piers and skeleton of arches standing on the platform at the centre of a lake. A stone bridge connects the tomb with the mainland.

Shar Shah entered Delhi in 1540 as the new ruler. He is believed to have founded Sher Garh, a new city, around the ancient site of Indraprastha. It is now remembered only by the two gateways built on the city boundaries. Lal Darwaza, near the Purana Qila, is a mammoth structure in red sandstone dressing over the local quartzite. The road under it is lined up with ruins of small apartments, perhaps a market place. Hugh bastions on strong fortifications flank the impressive gateway which has a high, pointed-arch entrance.

Khuni Darwaza, the other gateway on Sher Garh walls, stands near Kotla. It is a grim and formidable double-storeyed structure with in-built rooms for guards. It is chiefly remembered as the scene for the enactment of many a dramatic and blood curdling scenes of cruelty typical of the medieval times.

The walls, ramparts and three magnificent gateways of the fort were completed by Humayun during his stay in Delhi before he lost his throne to Sher Shah in 1540. The Bada Darwaza, main entrance on the western wall, is massive gateway. The arched entrance is protected by two rounded bastions flanking it. Talaqi Darwaza, on the northern side, and the Humayun Darwaza, on the southern side, are the other two magnificent gateways of the fort, now generally referred to as the Purana Qila. It is believed that both Kotla and Siri ruins provided the stones for the building of this fort.

The Purana Qila does not contain many structures. Humayun had little time to embellish it with places and towers etc.

The Qala-i-Kuhna Masjid (mosque in the Purana Qila) (1542) is the only structure in the fort assigned with certainty to Sher Shah. Here in culminates the architectural style of the Lodi mosque. It is a much-improved version of the Jamali Kamali Masjid in matters of harmonising various architectural components and surface ornamentation. It is not a large structure. The single bay prayer hall measures 51.20m by 14.90m.

The five-arched façade is extremely elegant. Each arch is set within a larger recessed archway. A rectangular frame, with narrow turrets on either side has fluted mouldings inspired by stellate flanges of the Qutb Minar. These turrets culminate in small pinnacles rising over the corner of the central arch.

The central arch has received the maximum ornamentation. It has a lotus bud fringe, and rosettes on spandrels. An oriel window is set within panels inlaid with marble and coloured stones. The central mihrab is a masterpiece of craftsmanship in stone, the forte of Indian artisans whose consummate skill matched the jeweller's precision and artistry. The treatment of the imposts, foliation of the arch, elegant borders and a masterly finish by sinking one arch into another recessed arch, multiplies the scope for lavish ornamentation. The ceiling in the prayer hall shows recourse to three styles in the 'phase of transition' the squinch, stalactite and semi-vault of an unusual design.

The rear portion of the mosque is also part of careful planning of various structural features. Two triple-storeyed semi octagonal towers with arched balconies over heavy ornamental brackets add strength and grace to the structure. The unmistakable taper of turrets in the Tughlaq architecture appears here at the turrets on the rear aspect of the central bay in the prayer hall. The Qala-i-Kuhna Masjid is believed to have had three domes. Only the central hemispherical dome has survived

to this day. A marble tank lies at the centre of the courtyard. This mosque, certainly, is the last step towards the magnificent mosques typical of Mughal grandeur.

In 1547 Isa Khan, an Afghan chief of Sher Shah's army, built for himself an octagonal tomb, near the Humayun Tomb area. It is enclosed within formidable walls. The structure, more ornate that other octagonal tombs in Delhi, lacks height. The plinth is rather low for such a structure. The superstructure is crowded with eight chhattris and pinnacles over the chhajja and the parapet is lined with merlons. The dome is crowned with a lotus finial. The tomb carries traces of decoration with blue and green tiles. Within the extensive garden enclosure of the Isa Khan's tomb is a small mosque with triple pointed arches and decoration with brilliant colourful inlaid tiles. The central dome is flanked by two large chhattris which is quite a new structural element providing elegance and variety to the simple and modest mosque.

Sher Mandal, the octagonal double-storeyed tower in red sandstone, near the mosque, was perhaps used as a small palace. It is surmounted by an octagonal chhattri. The ground floor rooms are sealed because herein was kept Humayun's corpse before final burial at his tomb built by Akbar. On the first floor the rooms are arranged in cruciform with restrained decoration in glazed tiles. This tower was used as a library by Humayun and the young Akbar received his early lessons in painting from Mir Syed Ali, one of the two painters brought to India by Humayun from Persia. In books of history Sher Mandal is known as the tower from whose steps Humayun fell down as he knelt down in prayer. His feet got entangled in the dress, causing his fall. He was mortally wounded in this accident on January 24, 1556 and died after three days.

Controversy surrounds the authorship of Purana Qila ramparts, gateways and Sher Mandal but both Sher Shah and Humayun were at ease with the architectural style which only followed the time-honoured traditions of fort building since the beginning of the Delhi Sultanate in Delhi. Both had no time for pursuing architectural ambitions though both cherished to be remembered as great builders. The Mughals had arrived on the scene, but took their own time to make a statement of their architectural designs. It was Akbar who did it.

facing page. The Mihrab in white marble at the mosque of Sher Shah, Delhi.

top right. Mosque of Sher Shah, Delhi.

right. Sher Mnadal at the Purana Qila, Delhi.

13
THE
GREAT MUGHALS
BABUR, HUMAYUN & AKBAR

There are but a few structural remains of the buildings of both Babur and Humayun because of their ceaseless military campaigns throughout northern India. Besides, Babur who chose to stay in Agra never really liked India. He hated the climate, landscape, fruits and people. Samarqand and Herat remained his dream cities. The Timurid mosques, tombs, madarsas and gardens fascinated him. Babur did not even like to be buried in India. It had to be in Kabul. He created a Kabul in Agra for his Samarqandi and Khurasani nobles and compatriots by developing the eastern bank of the Yamuna into a range of Persian gardens and mansions. If he could create a garden out of this inhospitable land he could create an empire. Babur actually did so. He created the Mughal empire which lasted nearly three hundred years.

left. Humayun's Tomb, Delhi.

above. Babur supervising the building of a pond in a garden.

In Agra, Babur built Gul Afshan, the first Mughal Char bagh in India. The *hisht bihisht* or four-quartered garden of eight paradises on the eastern bank of the river, occasionally mistaken for the present Ram Bagh but recently identified with some ruins facing the Taj Mahal. Here, Babur held his court and parties. The garden had baths, tanks, audience hall and private apartments fed with an inexhaustible supply of running water harnessed through Persian wheels and stepped wells. He sat under grand awnings. The garden was built in the image of paradise.

Babur also built a lotus garden Bagh-i-Nilufar, amid rocky and nearly barren surroundings near Gwalior. It is now survived by a few ruins, water channels, bath, well and the lotus-shaped stone pool. He also a garden and *baoli* near Sikri following his victory over the Rajput chief Rana Sanga in 1527.

The mosque at Sambhal (1526) is the first mosque built under the Mughals. Mir Hindu Beg, who served both Babur and Humayun, built this impressive mosque over a high prominence. The pishtaq is very high and wide. The mosque has three-bayed, double-aisled side wings, and a single dome over the sanctuary. Two small corner towers distinguish this first mosque of the Mughal period. It has been much repaired but remains in use to this day.

Babur built a mosque in Panipat (1528-29) where he had comprehensively beaten Ibrahim Lodi in 1526. This is a brick structure covered with stucco. The rectangular sanctuary is domed and flanked by a three bayed triple-aisled side wings. Massive piers support arches. Only one of the two octagonal towers, built at both ends of the facade, has survived. The mosque follows the architectural style of the Lodis. The only new feature is the use of net pendentives as an ornamental device on the zone of transition, a pseudo-structural plaster relief work applied to the pendentives of the small domes of the lateral bays. It provides a continuous network below the dome. The actual construction in brick or stone behind the plaster is corbelled. The mosque is much ruined but the pishtaq looks very impressive.

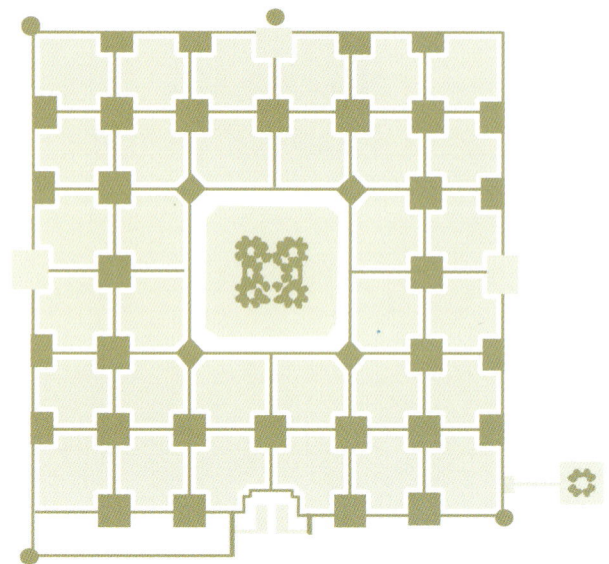

top. Layout plan of Kachpura Mosque, Agra.

above. Layout plan of Humayun's Tomb, Delhi.

right. Babur's mosque in Panipat, Haryana.

facing page. Detail of ceiling from Humayun's tomb, Delhi.

The third Baburi mosque at Ayodhya has been destroyed (1992). It was single-aisled and three-bayed structure with a high pishtaq virtually relegating the central dome out of view.

Humayun's mosque at Kachpura, near Babur's garden area in Agra was built in 1530. Believed to have been modelled after the Namazgah Mosque in Qarshi near Samarqand, this mosque has a grand pishtaq rising high over the side wings. The wings have crumbled but the archnetting in the transitional zones is still clear. Built in brick, covered with stucco, this mosque had very little ornamentation but a new predilection for openness and space is all too evident. The real impact of the new Persian concepts of architecture had to wait for nearly three decades before making an impressive appearance in Delhi.

In 1530, Humayun fell seriously ill and his death became a near certainty. Babur, extremely vexed over the misfortune, offered to make any sacrifice to save the life of the ailing prince and heir. When it was suggested that he sacrifice Kohinoor, his prizest possession, he ventured further and offered his own life. He went round Humayun's bed thrice, muttering to himself "O God! If a life may be exchanged for a life I, who am Babur, give my life and my being for Humayun". Babur's prayer was answered. Babur had "borne it away". Humayun recovered his health and Babur soon fell ill and died within a few months. Some, however, ascribe Babur's death to the effects of poison given to him by Ibrahim Lodi's mother. Before his death, Babur extracted a promise of Humayun: "If God should grant you this throne and crown, do not put your brothers to death but do carefully look after them". Both the crown and his brothers gave Humayun endless troubles till he lived.

In 1555, only a few months after he had regained the crown of Delhi, Humayun fell down the steps of Sher Mandal in Purana Qila. His robe got entangled as he sat down to pray and tumbled down. He broke his skull and finally died three days afterward on January 26, 1556.

The tomb of Humayun was built by his widow Hamida Banu Beghum. Designed by Mirak Mirza Ghiyas from Persia, this great tomb is built on a monumental scale, first example of the magnificent Mughal architecture. Some of its features-the garden setting and double dome had already made an appearance at Sikandar Lodi's tomb. Here the grand scale of the building transforms every structural element into sheer splendour.

The Humayun Tomb stands within an enclosed char bagh, a replica of a paradise, divided into four equal sections and further divided by parterres and narrow water channels reviving memories of mountain springs, so loved by the Mughals. Entrance to the tomb garden was provided through a gateway on the southern wall, now closed. The western gateway is in use presently. The whole structure of the tomb is raised on a one

metre high platform. A 7m high plinth in red sandstone containing 124 vaulted chambers and 17 arched cells on each face of the square forms the first stage of construction. On this prominent terrace stands the grand tomb. It is octagonal in plan, crowned by a 38m high slightly bulbous dome in marble. At the centre of each side is a porch 12.2m high with a pointed arch, flanked by outer bays with a similar pointed-arched entrance. The smaller arched recesses are covered with splendid jali screens in stone and marble. Throughout, the facade shows a judicious and artistic use of white marble in outlining arches, panels and rosettes and six-pointed stars. The blending of red sandstone with white marble creates a very pleasing effect of contrasting planes and deep shadows, attempted earlier at the Alai Darwaza and the tomb of Ghiyasuddin Tughlaq. Here the magnificent proportions of the structure fully illustrate advantages of polychromatic ornamentation.

The interior of the Humayun tomb follows the nine-fold plan of construction. The corners of the square are chamfered forming an irregular octagon, called Muthamman Baghdadi by the Mughals. The four intersecting lines divide the space into nine sections, the domed chamber lies at the centre, rectangular open sections in the middle of each side accommodate the pishtaqs or pillared verandahs, and the corner rooms are double-storeyed and vaulted seen as vaulted niches (nashiman) on the facade. As further refinement of this arrangement, additional diagonal passages link the corner rooms to the central chamber in a radially planned version. The eight rooms around the central chamber form the hisht bihisht or eight paradises. This plan with suitable alterations was to become an important part of the Mughal architecture. Under the nine-fold plan the tomb structures have domes and residential palaces have one or more chattris on the flat roof.

The double-dome at the Humayun tomb is in the authentic Persian tradition with a hollow between the outer and the inner shell. The inner shell rises to a height suitable to the interior of the cenotaph chamber below. The outer shell of masonry is constructed at the height governed by the total conception of the elevation. The dome at this tomb has a slightly constricted neck and high pitch with the finial rising directly from the apex without any intervening structural element in the Persian tradition. The rooms built around the drum of the dome were used for the madarsa. Pinnacles and chhattris built in the indigenous fashion, happily incorporate a few ornamental features from the architectural repertoire of the Delhi Sultanate into the geometrically correct and punctliously executed Persian design. The Humayun tomb remains the most magnificent tomb in Delhi, second only to the Taj Mahal in Agra.

The Humayun tomb was the only royal structure built by

top. Tomb of Atagha Khan at NIzamuddin, Delhi.

below. Sabz Burj, near Humayun's Tomb, Delhi

facing page. Building of Agra Fort. Mughal Miniature from the Akbarnama, *courtesy Victoria & Albert Museum, London*

Akbar in Delhi. The other smaller buildings do not represent the great Mughal style but a mere continuation of the prevalent Lodi style of the Sultanate. The Khairul-Manazil Masjid and Madarsa (1561) built by Maham Angha, Akbar's wet nurse, stands close to the Purana Qila. It is a rubble-built structure with a five arched screen in front of the sanctuary. Originally the mosque was embellished with green and yellow enamelled tiles. The double storeyed cloisters and the impressive gateway in red sandstone speak well of her influence at the court. An unsuccessful attempt on young Akbar's life was made near this mosque.

Within the Nizamuddin Dargah stands the small tomb of Atgah Khan, husband of Ji Ji Angha, another wet nurse of Akbar. Adham Khan, son of Maham Angha killed Akbar's favourite Atgah Khan in 1566. The tomb is a small gem of architecture. On all four sides of this square tomb are deeply recessed arches. The whole structure is covered with inlaid marble and coloured tiles. Built as a small replica of the Humayun Tomb this tomb in red sandstone served as precursor of lavish surface decoration at Akbar's tomb at Sikandara, near Agra.

The Sabz Burj, near the Humayun tomb, is known for its green tile decoration on the high neck dome. The structure displays the execution of the nine-fold plan on a small scale. This tomb belongs to the early Mughal phase, perhaps preceding the Humayun tomb. It is built in the Central Asian tradition which had but little influence on the local, indigenous architectural style. The identity of the person buried here remains unknown.

Within the Humayun tomb complex is Arab Serai, with a lofty gateway. Herein were housed the 300 Persian artisans specially brought by Humayun's widow to work on the tomb of her husband. The Afsarwala mosque and tomb stand together on a platform in the Arab Serai enclosure. The mosque has three arched openings with a single dome over the central bay. The small octagonal tomb has a double dome. The authorship of these structures, built in 1566-67, remains open to conjecture.

Adham khan, Akbar's foster brother who had killed Atgah Khan in 1566 was buried in an octagonal tomb, built close to the Qutb Minar. It is built on a podium in grey sandstone. The tomb has earned some fame for its maze of passages built within the corona of the dome. Adham Khan's brother, Muhammad Quli Khan, was also buried south of the Qutb. This tomb is now only remembered as the only tomb converted into a country house by Charles Metcalfe, a British resident. He made a few necessary alterations in the structure to suit his requirements. This is the last octagonal tomb to be built in Delhi, the culmination of the trend started by Khan-I-Jahan Tilangani during 1388-89.

The tomb of the Sufi saint Nizamuddin was provided with the present octagonal drum and dome in 1562. Humayun had also added a tablet at the adjacent tomb of Amir Khusro, Nizamuddin's favourite disciple and first poet in the Urdu language. Outside the northern-eastern corner of the Humayun tomb are the structural remains of the rooms with verandahs where Nizamuddin, Delhi's most venerated sufi saint, lived an practised austerities. Chilla-Nizamuddin Auliya, now extremely

واز اساس پس تاکنکده بسپکهائی لاشیده سرخ تراشیده که یکی درصفاآمیه کیتنی ناودرنگ کلکنده خساراقبال توا...

جنان بهم وصل یافت که مروی را ودرفران راه نبود واین حصا عالی که مثال بهند پس خال بندیده درع...

Layout plan of Agra Fort with labels: Delhi Gate, Hathi Pol, Moti Masjid, Yamuna, Diwan-i-Am, Jahangiri Mahal, Amar Singh Gate.

facing page. Gateway at the Agra Fort.

below. Jahangir Mahal, Agra Fort.

below right. Bengali Pavilion at Agra Fort.

right. Layout plan of Agra Fort.

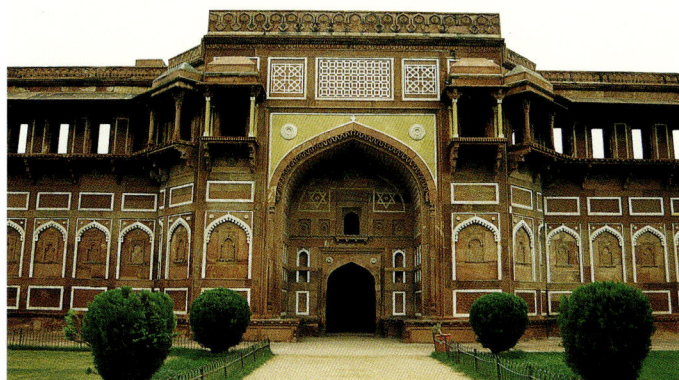

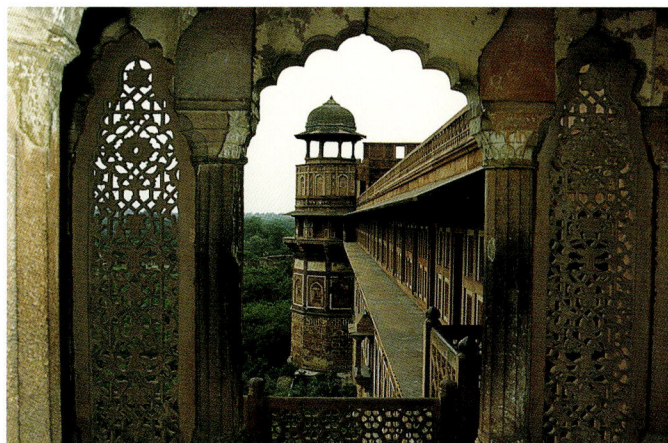

dilapidated, provides spiritual succour to Humayun, who lies buried close to the saint's house.

THE FORT-AGRA

In 1565, Akbar made his final break from Delhi. He rejected the former imperial capital of the sultanate in assertion of his authority, reducing associations of legitimate rulership with Delhi. No longer was it to be believed that he who ruled Delhi, ruled India. He ordered construction of a great new fort at the site of Badalgarh, the mud fort of Sikandar Lodi. Qasim Khan Mir, Barr-u-Bahr, was appointed supervisor of the work, planned by mathematicians and able architects. Solid foundations were laid with excavations made "through seven strata of earth". The whole magnificent structure of the fort was covered with red sandstone, as "ruddy as the cheek of fortune", as Abul Fazl recorded in the court chronicles.

The plan of the fort is an irregular semi-circle with its chord lying parallel to the course of the Yamuna river flowing below the stupendous ramparts, rising 22m in height. The walls have a circumference of nearly 2.5km punctuated with broad and massive bastions, battlements, embrasures, machicolations, string courses and such other features which contributed strength to the massive, impregnable fort.

The fort has two mammoth gateways. The Delhi Gate was the first to be completed during 1568-69. It is a monumental gate with impressive circular bastions flanking the grand arched entrance. These part-octagonal bastions are double-storeyed structures, with rooms for guards. Battlemented parapets and elegant chattris add to the splendour of the exterior which has been decorated with oblong panels outlined with white marble and geometrical and conventionalised designs of birds and animals. Now closed to visitors, the Delhi Gate is a grandiose structure of the new Mughal power. Akbar, very fond of elephants, installed a pair of gigantic elephant statues with riders on both sides of the central arch, in honour of Jaimal and Phatta,

left. Brackets sculptured in Hindu Style, Jahangir Mahal, Agra Fort.

below. Jahangir Mahal, interior, Agra Fort.

facing page. Slender and elegant Persian columns at the Agra Fort.

defenders of the Chittaur Fort, conquered by Akbar. Later on Aurangzeb had these statues removed and destroyed.

Akbari Gate, presently called Amar Singh Gate, on the western ramparts, is equally magnificent. It has a drawbridge over the wide moat girdling the ramparts, a crooked entrance with dangerous trap points and a steep incline to arrest fast movements of troops. The Naubat Khana, from where the drummers announced entry of the emperor, is an extremely impressive high structure with polygonal towers ornamented with blue enamel tiles. The pillared pavilions over this gate add a certain delicate elegance to the structure.

Abul fazl mentions that originally the Red Fort had nearly 500 buildings of the Gujarati and Bengali designs. Except these two mammoth gateways and two smaller gates opening towards the river front, the only surviving structures built by Akbar are a few ruins of the Bengali Mahal on the southern ramparts and the Jehangiri Mahal. Almost all other buildings were pulled down by

Jehangir and Shahjahan to provide space for new palaces and pavilions in white marble in contrast to the red sandstone used on Akbari buildings.

The Jehangiri Mahal is a large impressive palace, presumably meant for the royal harem. Reached through an impressive gateway: a large iwan, decorated with panels of geometrical mosaic in white marble. The whole facade is covered with a blind arcade of bud-fringed pointed arches. These semi-octagonal towers flanking the iwan are topped with oriel windows or jharokhas. A wide chhajja runs across the upper section below the parapet leading to elegant chhattris on both corners. The exterior of the Jehangiri Mahal sets the tone of the architectural style followed here: it is an essentially Islamic scheme of a symmetrical ground plan modified with the insertion of a few indigenous decorative elements.

The open courtyard inside is surrounded by grand rectangular halls with trabeated entrances. The Jehangiri Mahal

above. Govind Deva temple in Brindavan, Uttar Pradesh.

is a veritable show case of Indian stonecutter's consummate artistry. The brackets supporting the heavy chhajjas are extremely well covered and, for their prodigality, appear more an ornamental feature then a structural expedient. The hall in the northern section has a flat ceiling supported on diagonal struts. The brackets are serpentine in form. The whole upper storey has a surfeit of these brackets, an exhibition of over-spirited virtuosity in craftsmen from Gujarat and Malwa trying to surpass the sculptural decoration at Man Mandir at the Gwalior Fort, the original source of inspiration. Both Babur and Akbar admired the skill of Indian stonemason. Akbar allowed his craftsmen full freedom to exhibit his art. The result is an extremely amazing variety of brackets, exquisite and sensitive decoration on wall surfaces carved with the patience and finesse of a jeweller.

The Jehangiri Mahal also finds use for a number of vaulting styles-stucco domes with geometrical patterns and arch netting, ribbed domes and lotus domes carved in sandstones, pyramidal vault with a cut top, caved ceilings etc. Akbar's liberal attitude toward using indigenous decorative elements on structures of Persian inspiration brought about an admirable synthesis of both Indian and Persian forms of architecture.

The Persian features of architecture at the Jehangiri Mahal are no less brilliantly essayed. The arches are pointed and the *Chini Khana* (niches in walls for displaying vases and bottles) is exquisitely and correctly fashioned. The verandah on the eastern, river front side, has slender pillars in stone closely imitating the design and elegance of the wooden columns in Persian architecture. These triple openings on the verandahs lead to the sunken fountains in the open courtyard. The rectangular windows on the wall frame views of fascinating vistas on the river front.

Akbari buildings at the Lahore fort were nearly all pulled down by Jehangir and Shahjahan. The fort at Allahabad contains only one structure of importance. It is called Rani ka Mahal, a zenana palace which has received peristylar form of treatment. Built on the nine-fold plan, this pavilion has a grand columnar arrangement in groups of four columns at the corners and in pairs of two in the middle, a total of 96 splendid columns with fine capitals. The brackets are spectacular and the chhajja quite prominent. This palace is far superior to any other palace of its class, now closed to visitors. The double-storeyed stepped pavilion overlooking the confluence of rivers was perhaps still more enchanting but now survives only in a print of Thomas and William Daniell (Oriental Scenery, 1795-1808). The square central chamber has a trabeate construction adapted to an octagonal plan. The pillared verandah is topped by smaller version on the upper floor, crowned with a multifaceted chhattri covered with copper plates. Other versions of this pavilion can still be seen at the Akbari Mahal and Musamman Burj built by Akbar and Jehangir respectively in red sandstone and white marble at the Agra Fort. Except for the Rani ka Mahal, the Allahabad fort has no other building by Akbar.

The palace at the Ajmer Fort (1570) now houses the museum. It is also built on a nine-fold plan with rooms in corners and a verandah with triple openings in the middle of each side. The central hall has a flat ceiling. The corner rooms have windows with jali screens.

The Jaunpur Fort (1566) has been much repaired and altered. The entrance gateway, built by Akbar's governor Munim Khan, still stands with traces of original decoration with blue and yellow glazed tiles. The Akbari Bridge over the Gomti River is a more solid evidence of Mughal utilitarian architecture, still in use after more than four hundred years.

Two other forts-Chunar and Rohtas, built under the royal patronage, have some functional buildings, conspicuously lacking the grandeur of lavish construction and decoration which is the hallmark of Mughal architecture.

The fort at Chunar, over the Ganges, was built (1573-74) by Muhammad Sharif Ganges Khan son of Abdul Samad, one of the two painters from Persia, brought by Humayun. The gateway at the fort is particularly impressive for its strength and decoration carved panels, brackets and oriel window. The employment of local artisans has carried forward the influence of Sher Shah's architecture.

Contemporary trends in Mughal architecture did not much affect the Islamic architecture in Bengal. The Kherua Mosque (1582) has a brick-construction, uses curved cornice and engaged ribbed corner turrets. It is single bayed and triple-aisled. Inscriptions are in Persian, rather than in Arabic. This is the most impressive mosque in Sherpur. The Jami Masjid in Malda (1595-96) has an imposing brick structure covered with fine plaster as at the Kachpura mosque of Humayun. The Nim Serai Minar is a very interesting structure, resembling the Chor Minar, built by Alauddin Khilji, in Delhi. It is also decorated with elephant tusks. Perhaps it functioned as a watch tower. Or may be, the severed heads of culprits were hung here for public display.

The regional manifestations of architecture clearly show the effects of lack of funds and a fear of competing with the royal masters. Few buildings are in stone, and, almost all are built in rubble covered with plaster. The proportions are modest and lack innovation unlike what is seen in imperial constructions.

Raja Man Singh of Amber, Akbar's relative and most trusted general, built an impressive palace at Rohtas, the largest non-imperial palace in the Mughal empire. It has residential apartments, *baradari*, audience halls, *hammams* and *jharokhas* etc.

when transferred to Bengal, Man Singh built a grand Jami Masjid at Rajmahal, reminiscent of Babur's mosque in Panipat. But Man Singh's most important architectural contribution is the Govind Deva temple in Brindavan (1590). It is a magnificent edifice with very prominent horizontal mouldings and oriel windows. The arcuated vaults and domed interiors are ingeniously worked out. No less striking is the use of net pendentives, domes and barrel-vaults derived from the contemporary Mughal architecture. The red sandstone used for construction is comparable in quality to the fabric of Sikri palaces. The Govind Deva temple is the only temple to use genuine Islamic forms of construction so successfully.

The mosque at Nagaur (1564) built by Husain Quli Khan, is a very impressive structure. The Akbari mosque at the dargah of Muinuddin Chisti in Ajmer (1570) is remarkable for its high pishtaq, only a little less formidable than the pishtaq at Humayun's mosque in Kachpura, Agra. It is decorated with net pendentives and geometrical patterns.

The tomb of Muhammad Ghaus in Gwalior, built in red sandstone, is a precursor for the white marble tomb of Sheikh Salim Chisti at Sikri. The structure is borrowed from the Gujarat prototypes.

The tomb and water palace of Shah Quli Khan (1590-91) in Narnaul shows a clear link with imperial architecture. The water palace uses the nine-fold plan. It is an elegant building surrounded by an artificial lake, recreating the paradisal imagery associated with such pleasure pavilions. Man Singh built a similar water palace in Bairat, near Jaipur. The nine-fold plan has also been followed at Bada Batashe-wala Mahal (c.1603), tomb of Mirza Musharraf Husain, built near the tomb of Humayun in Delhi.

below: Floral relief on the wall of the Red Fort, Agra.

14

FATEHPUR SIKRI

There is some truth in the popular belief that Akbar built the city of Sikri in a gesture of thanks giving towards the renowned sufi saint Sheikh Salim Chisti. The emperor got three sons in realisation of the saint's blessings. But it was not only "to give outward splendour to this spot (Sikri) which possessed spiritual grandeur", as Akbar's historian Abu'l Fazl mentions. It was the decision of the young but astute empire builder. Akbar visited regularly the tomb and *dargah* of the first great sufi saint Muinuddin Chisti at Ajmer, the spiritual capital of Muslim India, called 'Qaba of the East', 300 miles away from his own capital Agra. Sikri was meant to bridge the gap and bring closer the spiritual and political capitals and, thus, add to his might the glory of the saint.

Akbar was also conscious of the power of his nobles and high officials. As Attilio Petruccioli observes, Sikri was "conceived as a seat for the court through an operation analogous to that a century later when Louis XIV established his court at Versailles, centralizing the court in order to keep the nobility firmly under control. It is perfectly possible that Akbar set about controlling the various ethnic groups (Rajputs, Turks, Afghans and Persians) who were continually at war with each other, by the simple expedient of uprooting them either from their territories or from an economic centre such as Agra. That Fatehpur Sikri is a residential city, 'a gilded prison' for the court, and not a redundant Agra, is demonstrated by the insufficiency of its military defenses". If this accounts for the shift to Sikri, it also explains why Akbar deserted it in favour of Lahore in 1585.

The imperial complex at Sikri is arranged in an echleon formation on the east-west axis on the ridge. It has an irregular layout. The hall of public audience forms the most important centre of this complex approached though the Agra Gate, markets and *karkhanas*. At the back of this public enclosure lies *mardana*, the royal area for the male population of the palaces. The royal *harem* or the *zenana* enclosure lies behind this.

Quite apparently, the Imperial Mughal architecture at Sikri follows the layout of Arab and Central Asian tent encampments. The palaces are built as separate, free-standing units in formal geometrics, on a piece of level ground, vastly different from the grouped-together style of the Rajput and Gujarat royal palaces. Here, as John F. Richards observes: "Akbar recreated in stone within the boundaries of Fatehpur Sikri, a comfortable and certainly grand encampment. It was an urban form somewhere between a camp and an imperial city", underlined by the uniform look created by the use of red sandstone.

The most striking feature of the architectural style Sikri is the use of trabeate construction known to Indians for centuries. The

Gujarati Sultanate architecture has an overwhelming influence over the architecture at Sikri to an extent that Ebba Koch calls it "Akbar's architectural response to the absorption of Gujarat into the Mughal empire". G.H.R. Tillotson notices this "process of Hinduisation" where "a few Islamic motifs remain as exotic details in a style in which the majority of the component parts are Hindu". Perhaps it was only a step towards achieving that social harmony which Akbar promoted through interaction with representatives of different religious groups. In any case, this admixture of Persian and Gujarati Sultanate style expresses Akbar's syncretistic genius, a new architectural style forged out of a unique combination of two vastly divergent architectural styles. Over all, however, the essential elements of town and structural planning remain consistently Islamic.

The Diwan-i-Aam, is the first royal building from the Agra Gate side. It stands within a large, open courtyard. It is a flat-roofed projected balcony secured within exquisitely fashioned *jali* screens. The courtiers and visitors assembled in front of the royal seat where the emperor sat in judgement over petitions. Akbar's favourite elephant immediately crushed to death the guilty. If the elephant refused the command thrice, the culprit was freed as innocent. The elephant was kept tied to a hook which still can be seen embedded in the ground.

The enclosure behind the Diwan-i-Aam contains some of the famous structures at Sikri. The Diwan-i-Khas is a small structure, externally double-storeyed but a high ceiling hall internally a hall with a high ceiling, crowned with four corner chhattris. A heavy chhajja supported on brackets provides shade over the windows. This hall contains the illustrious pillar at the centre of the floor with four passages radiating from its raised circular seat. This seat is upheld by thirty six voluted and pendulous brackets sculptured in the typical style of Gujarat, most frequently seen on brackets at minars attached to mosques in Ahmedabad. It is not functional architecture. May be, the emperor sat here for inspecting the jewels, or it was the royal seat used for listening to religious discourses by various groups, comprising Zoroastrians (Parsis), Jesuits, *pundits* and *mullahs*. It could have been the much mentioned Ibadatkhana which has so far remained unidentified. More probably, this had a symbolic function with the column symbolising the axis of the world of the Hindu cosmology and the emperor occupying the hub or focus of the supreme power on the pattern of the *mandalas*. The seating arrangement the emperor overlooking the groups below showed Akbar in a new perspective, commanding all that he surveyed.

Aankh Michauli, the erroneously called set of three inter-connected rooms near Diwan-i-Khas, was perhaps the treasury

and the small kiosk outside with ornate toranas (foliated arches) in the typically Jain sculptural tradition used for disbursement of salary. This is a multi-purpose structure.

The Anup *Talao*, water tank with four stone bridges radiating from its central raised platform resembles the conception of the enigmatic grand pillar in Diwan-i-Khas. Akbar had the tank filled up with gold, silver and copper coins for distribution amongst the poor.

Overlooking the water tank stands a three-roomed pavilion, wrongly ascribed to Turkish Sultana. Every inch of surface on the walls has been carved in the most luxuriant fashion. The dado panels are the most beautiful specimens of naturalistic carving-animals, birds, flowers, palm trees and other vegetation.

The *Daftar Khana* stands on a platform of piers and arches with a façade of paired columns with bracketed capitals and chhajja. The bases of the columns are fashioned to resemble double peacock's tail. The spacious Pachisi Court lies at the northern section of the sprawling paved courtyard. The emperor is believed to have played Pachisi, essentially an indoor game, with slave girls as living pieces.

The Daulat Khana, part of the emperor's lodgings near the Anup *Talao*, comprises a set of rooms on the first floor and spacious cloisters on the ground floor. The concept of the structure is essentially Persian. This type of Pavilion with a central block raised above its surrounding verandah is a comparatively new structural addition to architecture at Sikri. The vault of the inner chamber (typical for Fatehpur Sikri is the ribbed coved ceiling, a convenient vaulting for rectangular halls) was -as usual in secular structures-concealed on the outside by a flat roof. This design appears mainly on buildings reserved for the emperor. The Diwan Khana-i-Khas and the Khilawatkada-i-Khas (Khwabgah) are two important sections of the emperor's private lodgings, connected with other palaces with long corridors, still surviving at a few places.

The famous Ibadatkhana remains untraceable. However, Rizvi and Flynn identify it with ruins close to the eastern gateway to the Jami Masjid: "a tumbled mass of rubble scattered with gravestones and scrubby trees…a massive rubble platform, 19.50 metres square, covered with about 18 cm of lime mortar, visible at the edges…a second platform, heaped upon this is more rubbish, which might represent a third platform". Suggestively, the Mughal miniature depicting this place shows domes in the background.

Haram Sara or the female quarters lie behind the *mardana* enclosure. Jodha Bai's palace is the chief palace which housed the princesses from Rajput states Amber, Bikaner, Jaisalmer, Marwar, Merta and Dungarpur etc. The main entrance is a double-storeyed structure. The central archway has a lotus-bud fringe. Overhead is a corbelled balcony. Heavily guarded, this entrance leads through a dark vestibule, to a spectacular courtyard surrounded by double-storeyed pavilions. Ornamentation in the typical Gujarati and Rajasthani styles is a striking feature of this palace-bell and chain motif, rosettes, pellets and niches in the walls to house images of deities. The columns are equally well embellished-square at the base, then octagonal, sixteen-sided and finally circular. Richly sculptured brackets below the chhajja are an indispensable part of the ornamentation. Roofs on the upper rooms on the northern and southern wings are covered with azure blue glazed tiles from Multan.

Mariam's Palace or *Sunehra Makan* belonged to Akbar's mother, Hamida Beghum, widow of Humayun, titled Mariam Makani. The faint traces of gold murals have earned this name for the structure which is extremely elegant. The central location of this palace in the female quarters shows the importance of its occupant.

Panch Mahal, a five storeyed stepped pavilion meant only for the enjoyment of royal ladies, stands close to Sunehra Makan. It is a remarkable structure built entirely on elegant columns. The ground floor contains 84 pillars (each differently carved); the first storey has 56 pillars, and the second storey has 20 pillars, and the third storey has 12 pillars. The top most storey has four pillars supporting a chhattri. There are 176 pillars, originally the space between pillars was filled up with perforated screens in stone. The structure has suffered much damage and the jalis have disappeared. Still, the Panch Mahal is a masterpiece of architecture, an essentially Persian concept of the *badgir* (wind-catching high tower) transformed into a pleasure pavilion for ladies.

Behind the Panch Mahal lie remains of a ladies garden, bath and small mosque. At the northern section of the *haramsara* is the most exquisitely ornamented, double-storeyed structure used by, in all likelihood, by Akbar's senior queens. Completed in 1571,

facing page, top. Diwan-i-Khas, Sikri.

below. Ornate pillar at Diwan-i-Khas.

this page, top. Interior of Jodha Bai Palace.

below. Anup Talao and Daulat Khana.

left. Panch Mahal, Sikri.

right. Jami Masjid, Sikri.

Hathi Pole, the grand ceremonial entrance to the palaces, lies north of the harem area. It is guarded by two elephant statues on high stone pedestals flanking the arched entrance. This portion of Sikri is the only depicted with recognisable faithfulness in contemporary Mughal miniatures. Later day, occupants of the city damaged these statues just as they severely damaged the dado panels at the so-called Turkish Sultana's palace, near the Anup Talao.

Hiran Minar, a tower in memory of Akbar's favourite elephant, studded with a thousand tusks in stone, stands on a high platform on the bank of the lake. The water reservoir in this area is still a fair state of preservation. The Hiran Minar, perhaps, functioned as the starting point for the Kos minars between Sikri, Agra and Delhi. The ruins of a magnificent caravanserai, stables, schools and a grand mansion occupied by Akbar's favourite historian Abul Fazl and his brother Faizi, a poet of distinction, are lined up on the ascent to the Jami Masjid section.

this palace has four rooms on the ground floor and two on the upper floor in a diagonal arrangement. The ornament is profuse; elegant and cirsp. Chhajjas and brackets register a dominant presence in the structural scheme. The geometrical patterns and the Islamic pointed arch on shallow arched niches find a place amidst luxuriant and exceptional decoration as seen on examples of woodcraft in Gujarat. The uniformly high standard of craftsmanship on red sandstone veneer creates its own splendour though according to G.H.R. Tillotson, ultimately it sums up as a "cabinet of curiosities". This "elaborate medley" of diverse architectural traditions achieves little which can be called new or original. The ornamentation here shows the concrete effect of Akbar's liberalism towards Indian craftsmen and it is quite unlikely that the Mughal emperor sought to make any political statement by bringing together the best of two different architectural traditions. This high-plinthed palace was perhaps connected with the other palaces through corridors and vaulted passages, now lost. The extensive *zenana* complex is supposed to have housed nearly 5000 women queens, princesses, royal female guests (wives of nobles and dignitaries allowed a month's kingly hospitality), and armies of attendants and guards. Birbal's house, as this palace is mistakenly called, was an important section of the female quarters.

The Jami Masjid at Fatehpur Sikri, amongst the first few structures to be completed here, looked "the goodliest meskite of the East" to William Finch in 1611. It occupies an area of 89 by 20m within the enclosed grand courtyard. The high pishtaq is a magnificent architectural creation flanked by arched openings. The whole line over the parapet is topped by small elegant chhattris in place of domes as in mosques at Chanderi and Mandu. The mosque, believed to have been modelled after Bibi Khanum's mosque to Samarqand, owes as much inspiration to the architecture of the Delhi Sultanate - Jaunpur and Gujarat.

The interior of the mosque is covered with the most sophisticated ornamentation floral arabesques and ingenious geometrical patterns in brown, red, turquoise, black and white, a picture of sheer splendour.

The rectangular courtyard measures 109 by 133m, surrounded by cells for the devout on the east, north and east sides. *Badshahi Darwaza* provides entrance to visitors from the palace area. The mosque, work of the Indian craftsmen and artisans who created splendid palaces in the royal enclosure, is the most chaste and unmixed Islamic style as is apparent from the façade of pointed arches, restrained ornamentation on the pishtaq, and the majestic domes, despite the fact that the central dome remains obliterated by the high pishtaq.

From the very beginning of the construction of the mosque, Akbar remained personally involved with the progress of the work. Later on, he paid much attention to various services at the mosque. It is recorded that Akbar occasionally swept the floor and gave *azan* (call for prayer). On June 26, 1579 Akbar himself read the *khutba*, written in Persian by Faizi. This was a great innovation, earlier attempted only by Timur and Mirza Ulugh Begh. Akbar concluded with the meaningful incantation " Allahu Akbar" meaning both ' God is Great' and 'Akbar is God'. More than the words, the gesture had tremendous impact. The orthodox elements were clearly sceptical of notions like the ones advanced by Faizi: "The old fashioned prostration is of no advantage to thee-see Akbar and you see God".

Sheikh Salim Chisti died on February 14, 1572. Eight years after his death, Akbar built the saint's tomb within the precincts of the mosque. Structurally, the tomb is an adaptation of similar tombs in Gujarat and Malwa. It has an inner domed chamber surrounded on all sides by a verandah of four straight walks to serve as ambulatory passage. The *jali* screens covering the wide openings in the verandah provide privacy and protection, and contribute architectural splendour as at the tombs of Shah Alam in Ahmedabad, Sheikh Ahmad Khattu in Sarkhej and Sheikh Muhammad Ghauth in Gwalior. Originally the tomb was only in red sandstone with sparse marble work. It was completely covered with marble by Qutbuddin Khan in 1606, on orders from Jehangir. The *jali* screens are specimens of fabulous craftsmanship in marble. The serpentine brackets in the porch have an amazing gracefulness. But the *piece de resistance* at the tomb is the ebony frame over the cenotaph fully covered with mother-of-pearl decoration. The crypt containing the real grave of the saint is sealed. There is no way to the top of the tomb. The dome acquired its marbles casing only in 1866. People of various faiths from distant countries visit Sikri to offer their homage to Sheikh Salim Chisti, if only to remind us : "Then king is dead, there's another king/ and one more king is another reign. King is forgotten, when another shall come: Saint and martyr rule from the tomb".(T.S.Eliot).

Behind the white marble tomb of the saint stands the *zenana rauza*, housing graves of the Sheikh's female family members. Originally, here the emperor and his ladies sat before the saint, witnessing the *sama*, an integral part of the Chisti faith incorporating musical performance leading to mystical ecstasy. The adjacent bigger structure is the *Jamat Khana* where the saint's disciples lived together. It now houses their graves.

In 1573, Akbar built the *Buland Darwaza*, the most spectacular gateway in the history of Indian architecture, on the southern wall of the mosque enclosure. The gateway celebrates Akbar's

victory over *Khandesh*. The towering portal has a height of
53.3m from the ground level. The architectural style is Persian.
It is semi octagonal in plan with the bevelled corners projecting
over the enclosing wall of the mosque. The high arched recess
in the centre is the dominant structural element. The arch is
bud-fringed, with large rosettes in the spandrels.

Over the parapet on the front are 13 small-arched openings
behind which stand 13 small chhattris. Three larger chattris built
in the Gujarat-Rajasthan tradition add crowing splendour to this
mammoth edifice. The overall decoration on this monument is
sober. One of the inscriptions on the gateway reads: "The world
is but a bridge: pass over but build no houses on it".

Behind the western wall of the mosque lies a cluster of
uncelebrated, unfrequented ruins. The Rang Mahal where Salim
was born; Stone Cutter's Mosque built by craftsmen who built
the palaces and the mosque; the much rebuilt house where
Sheikh Salim lived before moving into the mosque. Here also
can be seen the original models of the serpentine brackets on the
stone cutters's mosque. At the extreme north-western edge of
the ridge stands the Hada Mahal, a royal pleasure pavilion
topped by a chhattri raised on slender columns. Todar Mal's
baradari, an octagonal pavilion built on the nine-fold plan, and
verandahs with triple openings on each side, stands on the
south-western end of the ridge. The mosque and tomb of
Bahauddin looks like the tomb of Sheikh Salim Chisti but
with still more beautiful jali screens. It stands coutside the Tehra
Darwaza, shaded by a cluster of tamarind trees amid a rocky and
barren landscape.

*top, left. Exquisite craftsmanship on a
bracket at the Dargah of Sheikh Salim
Chisti, Sikri.*

*left, above. Baradari of Raja Todar Mal,
Sikri.*

left. Dargah of Sheikh Salim Chisti.

right. Buland Darwaza, Sikri.

15
Jehangir

The first architectural undertaking of Jehangir was the completion of Akbar's tomb. When Akbar died in 1605 the spade work on the tomb had already started. Jehangir took his own time to complete it. The tomb, situated in Sikandara, also called Behishtabad (abode of paradise), is one of the most innovative, if not exactly the greatest, tomb built for the great Mughals.

The tomb is surrounded by a large enclosing wall pierced by four gateways. The southern gateway provides the entrance to the Char Bagh, well laid out around the tomb. It is a magnificent gateway with a high central arch flanked by smaller arches on two levels. The structure raised on a small plinth draws attention for the superb intarsia work, decoration with geometrical patterns, large floral motifs and elegant inscriptional panels all in inlaid white marble and coloured stones on the red sandstone fabric of the structure. The inscriptions are designed by Abd'l Haqq Shirazi, later known as Amanat Khan who also worked on the Taj Mahal. The garden tomb is designed to reflect the glories of paradise. One of the inscriptions reads: " These are the gardens of Eden, enter them and live forever ".

The cubical structure of the gateway is crowned with four graceful minarets in white marble at the four corners. The first appearance of fully developed minarets on any Mughal building. This grand and monumental gateway is an independent architectural achievement and compares well with any similar structure built before or after it.

The large garden is divided into four sections with *khiyabans* (paved pathways). The tomb lies at the crossing of these paths. The gateways on the north, east and west walls face inward and their high *pishtaqs* seem to absorb these *khiyabans* into their voids.

The tomb is a large unconventional structure in five storeys. The first, ground storey with a 105m side, is an orderly and noble conception with arched recesses on all four sides, each containing a gloriously decorated iwan at the centre, topped by a graceful chattri in marble over the parapet. Above this ground floor rise three flat-roofed and arched storeys in a diminishing order, built in red sandstone. The fifth storey, built in white marble, is, in fact, an open terrace enclosed by an arcaded gallery fitted with carved jali screens and attractive chattris at the corners. At the centre lies the sarcophagus and a lampstand in white marble, carved with the ninety nine names of Allah.

Access to the grave of the emperor on the ground floor is provided through a vestibule on the central, southern iwan. The vaulted ceiling of this small cell, preceding the crypt chamber, is covered with the most exquisite frescoes in blue and gold. Presently, the crypt chamber is almost stark. The gold, silver, and Akbar's personal effects were plundered by the Jats in the late eighteenth century following the decline in the Mughal power and prestige.

In its present form, the tomb looks like a truncated pyramid. Scholarly opinion is divided over the need for a dome which, perhaps, could have provided the finished look. May be, the tomb was planned, like the Panch Mahal at Sikri, as a domeless, open-to-sky structure. Or, for sheer lack of interest in Jehangir who, at an advanced stage in the construction of the tomb, disapproved of much work already done, and ordered reconstruction by new engineers, the tomb could not be finished with the dome, if it was intended, as in most funerary structures. As it is, the whole structure lacks substance and qualities of unity and homogeneity. The middle storeys look too light and flimsy for their trabeated construction and frequent appearance of the chhattris. The whole elevation of Akbar's tomb suffers for want of the vision and imagination only a forceful personality could provide. Jehangir was temperamentally ill equipped to create architecture

left. Gateway at Akbar's tomb, Sikandara, Agra   above. Akbar's tomb at Sikandara, Agra.

of a superior high order. His interests lay in miniature painting and bird-watching, highly irrelevant to the art of building in stone.

Akbar's tomb was completed in 1612. This was the first major architectural project completed during Jehangir's rule. It gave clear indications of certain stylistic features soon to flower into maturer form under Shahjahan. The profuse use of white marble and coloured stones, stone intarsia, painted stucco and tile work as part of structural and decorational elements was an improvement on Akbar's reliance on red sandstone for all architectural undertakings. White marble, for its purity earlier used only on the tombs of saints, is used profusely on the top terrace of Akbar's tomb, minarets and decoration of the pishtaqs. White marble, which helps create the more Persianised appearance giving greater scope and prominence to ornamentation with precious stones, gradually replaces red sandstone during the reign of Jehangir.

More crucial to the development of architecture: "new solutions are tried out in the vaults. Characteristic are intricately patterned stucco vaults that fuse (or replace) the earlier arch-netting with a new pseudo structure network system developed from points (often stars) arranged in concentric circles. These patterns appear to have been inspired by Safawid sources (based in turn on Timurid forerunners), which became influential in this period. A typical feature of Jehangiri vaults is that the network generates fan-like formations of lozenge-shaped muqarnas. Another specific technique of lining domes almost exclusive to Jehangir's period is that of oversailing concentric tiers of small Timurid) inspiration, Ebba Koch's observations might answer why, at a later stage, the Mughal architecture became far-distanced and alienated from the indigenous traditions of architecture.

The tiered structure of Akbar's tomb shows some influence of the Shah Begam tomb in Khusro Bagh, in Allahabad. The tomb, built by Jehangir for his Rajput queen who died in remorse

at her son Khusro's rebellion against his father, was designed by Aqa Riza, the painter. It is in three tiers. The uppermost terrace is surmounted by a chhattri under which lies the sarcophagus and a vertical inscribed slab. This is not a massive or pretentious structure. But a simple trabeated structure in Chunar sandstone, completed in 1611.

The tomb of Sultan Nisar Begam, daughter of Jehangir, stands on a high podium. It has a high dome and the exterior is decorated with panels of scalloped arches. The interior is covered with paintings on stucco-wine vessels, floral motifs, geometrical designs and cypresses all of an unmistakable Persian inspiration.

The exterior of the tombs of Khusro is double-storeyed but internally it is a single large chamber. The heavy dome is surrounded by four chhattris at each corner. The interior is decorated with Persian motifs. Originally, a wooden canopy stood over the sarcophagus, suggesting Khusro's mass appeal as a saint, a reputation acquired for his sufferings, denial of the crown, blinding by Jehangir and ultimate death in 1621 while in the

the most respected queen of Akbar. This tomb continues the trend of light super-structures mounted on a high platform with vaulted bays or chambers.

The Kanch Mahal is a magnificent gateway leading to an unidentified octagonal tomb, near Sikandara. This double-storeyed gateway is, built on a nine-fold plan. The structure in red sandstone has lavish ornamentation with inlaid white marble. The decorative motifs included wine vessels and arabesques on the spandrels. Mutamad Khan's mosque in red sandstone also finds use for the wine vessel motif and geometrical patterns.

Meharunnisa, titled Nurmahal and later Nurjahan (light of universe), Jehangir's queen, was a celebrated beauty and an astute administrator. She headed the Parsian triumvirate at Jehangir's court. Mirza Ghiyas Beg, her father, fled the Persian court in utter penury. He is believed to have abandoned his new born daughter in the desert only for reasons of poverty. She, later restored to her parents, brought them good fortune. Ghiyas Beg rose to prominence under Akbar and later became Jehangir's chief

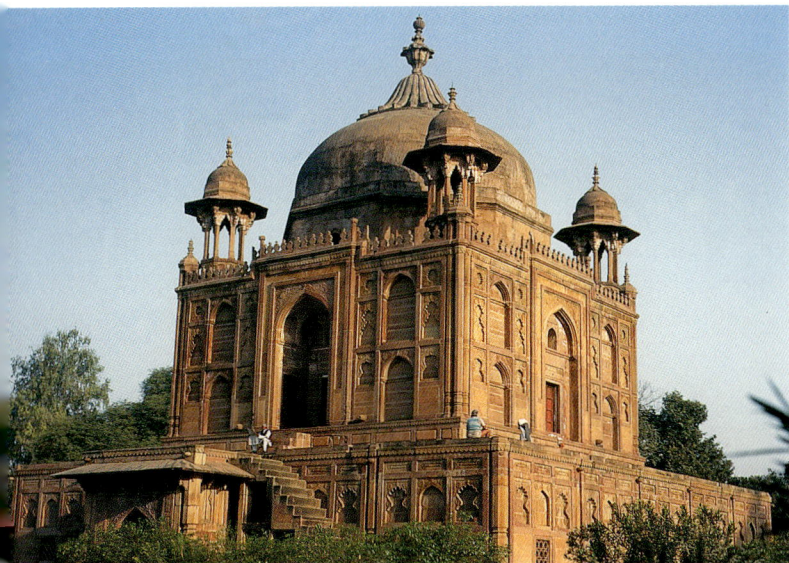

custody of Khurram, later Shahjahan.

The tomb of Tambulan Begam is built on an octagonal podium, containing a cruciform chamber. On the terrace is an octagonal domed chattri. The dome is built in the fashion, typical of the Jehangir period-network developed from stars arranged in concentric circles with lozenge-shaped muqarnas. In 1606 Aqa Riza also built the massive gateway to these garden tombs before working on Shah Begam's tomb. Akbar built this garden for Jehangir who gifted it to Khusro.

The tomb of Maryam Zamani, Jehangir's Rajput mother from Amber, stands near Akbar's tomb at Sikandara. It was perhaps a *baradari* of the preceding Lodi period. The exterior resembles the plinth of Humayu's tomb in Delhi while the interior is well planned and multi-chambered. The pavilion at the top has disappeared but the octagonal chhattris at corners and oblong ones over the centre of the four sides create the appearance of a royal structure befitting the occupant's status as

minister. Asaf Khan, her brother, was the other key member of this influential Persian group. On Ghiyas Beg's death in 1622 Nurjahan wished to build a mausoleum in memory of her father and mother Ghiyas Beg and Asmat Begam who predeceased her husband, in pure silver but which, for fear of thieves, was subsequently built entirely in white marble, the first of its kind in Mughal history.

The small tomb of Ghiyas Beg, titled Itmad-ud-daula (pillar of the sate) stands in an enclosed garden on the eastern bank of the Yamuna river near the garden built by Babur. Four gateways in redstone are built on the four sides. The eastern gateway, covered with splendid decoration, leads to the garden tomb. Raised on a modest plinth, the tomb is 70m in diameter. The cenotaph chamber is a rectangular ball surrounded by inter-connected rooms built on a simplified nine-fold plan. The vaulted ceiling is covered with the most gorgeous decoration on the roof and a square pavilion with a canopied dome forms the

right. Tomb of Itmad-ud-Daula, Agra.

above. Detail of pietra dura decoration at Itmad-ud-Daula, Agra.

modest superstructure. The pavilion looks rather overshadowed by the minarets. The *jali* screens on single slabs of white marble are, however, the most sophisticated and refined in craftsmanship. The graves are covered in green and yellow marble and the floor resembles an inlaid Persian carpet. Every aspect of this small tomb in marble speaks eloquently of Nurjahan's filial devotion and high aesthetics.

The tomb of Itmad-ud-daula, completed in 1628, is a remarkable tomb in the history of Indian architecture, not so much for its architectural features so much as for the stunning ornamentation on its exterior fully riveted in white marble. This is the first appearance in India of the pietra dura technique-use of precious and semi-precious stones like lapis, onyx, jasper, topaz and cornelian fashioned into recognizably Persian motifs of paradise-wine bottles, grapes, cypresses, medallions, the ubiquitous geometrical arabesque, and the still more adroitly worked floral scrolls inlaid into the sculptured hollows of the marble. The dazzle of the all-marble surface is considerably subdued by the subtle tints of the inlay. This variety of *pietra dura* is the culmination of the patterned mosaic (stone intarsia) earlier seen at the Qala-i-Kuhna mosque of Sher Shah in Delhi. The Italian pietra dura mainly relies on figurative work, imitating pictures in other media. The Mughal *pietra dura* is essentially ornamental.

These colourful stones were chosen by Nurjahan for the feel of their texture to create "an architecture of braille". The Itmad-ud-daula tomb marks the transition from red sandstone

structures of Akbari period to the era of architectural splendour in white marble ushered in by Shahjahan. It also shows how the Persianised motifs of ornamentation turned into an obsession with Jehangir and later Shahjahan.

Jehangir preferred long holidays in Kashmir and prolonged stays at Lahore where he made some structural additions and alterations to buildings at the fort. The Jehangiri Quadrangle has some chambers supported on brackets and pillars in the most functional and conventionalised order, distinguished for neither structural innovation nor for any ornamental feature. The ceiling at the Kala Burj has some Christian motifs-angels and birds, symbolising king Solomon's heavenly companions. The walls of the Lahore fort, built in brick, are decorated with tile mosaics depicting elephants, horses and camels engaged in combat.

The mosque of Maryam Zamani in Lahore (1611-12) is a five bayed and single-aisled building. The soffit of the central dome has a remarkable medallion with stellate and net forms in stucco, rendered in the characteristic style of ornamentation of the Jehangiri period.

It is, however, the small tomb of Anarkali (1611) which is a real gem of architecture. It is an "irregular octagon with arched octagonal towers at its points that project as half-octagons topped by octagonal chhattris a radial nine-fold plan with two patterns of cross axes (+ and x)." This most ingeniously planned octagonal tomb was for a while used as a Christian church in 1851 and now as an office of the government. The marble

facing page. A portion of the painted ceiling at Itmad-ud-Daula, Agra.

above. Layout plan of Itmad-ud-Daula.

cenotaph is covered with ninety-nine names of Allah inlaid in black stone in imitation of a similar inscription of God's names on Akbar's sarcophagus at Sikandara. Anarkali finds no mention in the court chronicles of Akbar. She was a slave girl of incredible beauty. Her torrid romance with Salim, the heir apparent hurt Akbar's vanity who had her walled in alive or simply had her whisked away to live in anonymity. Part of the inscription on her grave refers to "the profoundly enamored Salim, son of Akbar". She died in 1599. Curiously only two contemporary European visitors to the royal court Edward Terry (1616-1619) and William Finch (1608-1611) mention Anarkali by name. Both, however, call her one of Akbar's wives who had an illicit affair with Salim.

Jehangir was a great naturalist; loved nature, mountains, streams, birds and other unusual animals. He patronised miniature painting and lovely women, wine, opium and undiminished indulgences left him with little time for architectural projects. He was responsible for the ultimate appearance of confusion on Akbar's tomb. Itmad-ud-daula's tomb was built and supervised entirely by Nurjahan. The hectic building activity which characterised Akbar's rule slowed down considerably during Jehangir's rule. Architecture during his rule languished for want of a clear 'vision' and great noble ideas.

The flat-roofed, hypostyle hall with pillars or piers arranged in a grid pattern forms the core of many a tomb built during this period. The *Chausath Khamba* (1623) contains the grave of Mirza Aziz Kokaltash, son of Ataga Khan. This white marble pavilion in Delhi is similar to Salabat Khan's tomb, built in red sandstone, near Sikandara. The *Chausath Khamba* carries some exquisite *jali* screens on the arched façade of the tomb. Mihir Banu Agha, one of Jehangir's eunuchs built a bridge over a stream from the Yamuna river. It consists of eleven arched openings, but the twelve piers give it this name. Each pier is

surmounted by a 2m high turret. This bridge, still in use, stands behind the tomb of Abdul Rahim Khan-i-Khana, near Humayun's tomb.

Some of the smaller tombs deserve a mention for a certain type of architecture a central domed structure surrounded by a verandah on all sides. These are generally built on the nine-fold plan. The tomb of Makhdum Shah Daulat at Maner in Bihar (1616) is a notable tomb of this kind. The tomb of Iftikar Khan at Chunar (1612-1613) is an equally impressive structure. The most famous tomb of this period was built in Delhi. It belongs to Abdul Rahim Khan-i-Khana (1627). The tomb, perhaps of earlier origin, is built on a high arcaded podium. The cubical structure is topped by a high dome. All its marble decoration was removed for covering the tomb of Safdarjang in the 18th century. Still, this mere skeleton of the grand tomb is enough to prove that architectural trends, once accepted into the mainstream, mature in style with time. Built like the tomb of Humayun, Khan-i-Kahna's tomb served as model for the Taj Mahal.

The Serai Nur Mahal, near Jallundhar in Punjab, was built by Nurjahan (1618-1619). It has a stupendous gateway in red sandstone. The grand central arch is decorated with marble panels and oriel windows. It contained nearly 124 rooms and a mosque. The royal apartments were built on the southern wall. The other equally impressive serai was built by Itmad-ud-daula on the Lahore-Delhi route. The Serai Doraha built in 1610, is a brick structure containing a mosque and *hammam*. The two grand gateways on the north and south sides have large recessed arches framed within tile-worked rectangular panels.

Jehangir built a hunting lodge at Sheikhupura, near Lahore. His choice of picturesque setting for hunting lodges also led him to build another hunting lodge at the rocky outcrop, near Ajmer. Called Chasma-i-Nur, this lodge has an impressive *pishtaq* set within two sloping hillsides. The Pushkar pavilions, though mere rudimentary structures, served as royal resort on India's holiest lake. The octagonal reservoir and garden at Verinag in Kashmir has survived to this day with descendants of the large fish released by Jehangir still enjoying themselves in evergrowing numbers. Both the Shalamar and Nishat Bagh in Srinagar were built during this period. The emperor built the enchanting Shalamar, distinguished by two pavilions over the mountain spring channelised to feed the fountains and canals. The Nishat, built by Asaf Khan, brother of Nurjahan, exploits the slope of the mountains to create a terraced garden of stunning grandeur, much to the annoyance of Jehangir who hated to see anyone surpass his creations in beauty. Nurjahan is responsible for improving and adding to the structures at Aram Bagh, supposedly built by Babur in Agra. This was named Bagh-i-Nur Afshan, after the queen. With two oblong pavilions pools and a sunken fountain, the Bagh-i-Nur Afshan served as the queen's favourite garden for celebrations and parties. The pavilions still carry faint traces of the original paintings on stucco depicting the paradisical motifs of wine vessels and cypresses.

16

SHAHJAHAN

Mughal architecture reached its apotheosis during the rule of Shahjahan. There is a complete transformation in the building styles coupled with a change in the building material. The red sandstone, Akbar's favourite stone for Sikri and the Agra fort, was replaced by white marble now increasingly used with accentuated ornamentation in stone *intarsia* and *pietra dura*. The architecture during Jehangir's rule provided a fitting stage for this transition. Shahjahan chose white marble for its purity and splendour which sets off the building from its surroundings. His architecture, like his own stature as a semi-divine king, had to be a class by itself. The architectural ideals included emphasis on symmetry and uniformity. Enclosed areas housed the royal palaces for privacy, exclusiveness and security. Minarets now form an integral part of the architectural vocabulary. Use of *pietra dura* ornamentation on white marble adds grandeur characteristic of Shahjahan's architecture. Multi-faceted columns, baluster columns and curved roof are added to the structural idiom. The use of cusped or engrailed arch appears prominently on Shahjahan's buildings. The plant motifs, derived from European herbals, are used on dados and on column bases to highlight the paradisical imagery. The Mughals were charmed by the beauty of nature and they recreated it all around them on their architecture. Beside, plants and flowers symbolises the garden paradise, promised to the devout and the faithful by God. These naturalistically carved floral motifs, different from the figurative depictions of nature as seen on the dados at the so-called palace of Turkish Sultana in Sikri, are closest to Islamic ideals.

The first architectural project undertaken under Shahjahan's rule was the tomb of Jehangir at Shahdara, near Lahore. Jehangir, like Babur, wished to be buried in an uncovered grave. His tomb stands in a Char Bagh on a 84m single storeyed arcaded podium in red sandstone. The four minarets at the corners contribute grandeur to the edifice. The cenotaph on the terrace surrounded by *jali* screen has disappeared. The marble cenotaph in the interior of the podium is covered with elegant *pietra dura* and 99 names of God and the year of Jehangir's death.

left. Diwan-i-Aam, Agra Fort.   above. Marble pavilion on the Ana Sagar lake, Ajmer

Nurjahan's tomb (1645) is a square structure with seven arched openings on each side with no minarets. Her tomb, like the small octagonal tomb of Asaf Khan in the vicinity, is denuded of its surface decoration.

Shahjahan carried on large scale renovation at the Lahore fort. Buildings erected by Akbar and Jehangir, in red sandstone, were all pulled down. Musamman Burj was reconstructed. The Sheesh Mahal is a grand pavilion with a five-arched facade, supported on double marble pillars. This is the most magnificent palace at the fort with heavy ornamentation in *Aleppo* glass. *Naulakha*, a small pavilion with a deeply curved sloping roof, in imitation of thatched roofs in Bengal, was used for royal appearances. An inscription on the Elephant Gate describes Shahjahan as a 'Solomon in grandeur'. These images of royalty were to form a significant part of Mughal architecture under Shahjahan's patronage, emphasizing at every step the semi-divine status of the ruler.

The Diwan-i-Aam, reconstructed like its counterpart in the Agra Fort, has cusped arches introducing an acanthus leaf at the apex of the arches, a new decorative element. The whole structure is formal and majestic in appearance echoing Shahjahan's power and splendour.

The mosque of Wazir Khan (1634-35) is a single-aisled and five-bayed structure in bricks. The tile decoration at this mosque is glorious, unexcelled for its colour and splendour though its excessive use is not in keeping with the solemnity of mosque architecture. The Serai Dakhini built by Wazir Khan near Jullundhar, is also a massive and grand structure in bricks, covered with some elegant decoration in tiles.

facing page. Musaman Burj, Agra Fort.

right. Decorative pillar, Musamman Burj, Agra Fort.

below. Ceiling at Musamman Burj, Agra Fort.

Shahjahan completed work on the marble pavilions built on the Ana Sagar Lake in Ajmer. These are trabeated, flat-roofed structures supported by faceted columns and heavy ornamental brackets. There is an unmistakable look of classical purity in these small pavilions. The mosque, built by Shahjahan, at the *dargah* of the sufi saint Muinuddin Chisti also has the same look of austere grandeur. This eleven-arched mosque, a domeless structure with no pishtaq, is often compared to Kabba in Mecca. It is a grand but purely functional structure. Later on Shahjahan also added a large gateway to the dargah in 1655. Shahjahan, like his grandfather Akbar, kept his links with Islamic religious centres renewed by frequent visits to confirm his belief in orthodox Islam.

As at Lahore, in Agra Shahjahan began his architectural programme by dismatling palaces of Akbar and Jehangir, sparing only the Jehangiri Mahal the showpiece of Akbari architecture. He built new marble palace on the riverfront.

Diwan-i-Aam or *Chihil Sutun* (forty-pillar palace) was the first building entirely rebuilt in red sandstone covered with polished lime. Faceted pillars and cusped arches with acanthus leaves at the apex are grouped together to form a three-aisled, ten bay deep hall of public audience where the Mughal emperor appeared in all his splendour at the darbar. Nobles, rajas and high officials lined up in a rigidly enforced order of protocol. The nobles and rajas vied with each other to decorate areas in the hall allotted to them for this purpose.

The royal seat is triple-arched alcove of baluster columns inlaid with splendid and costly stones in the tradition of exquisite *pietra dura* ornamentation. The emperor sitting in this alcove presided over the proceedings in a grand manner likened to Solomon's seat of Justice. What is only suggested by court scribes is here tanslated into an architectural reality.

On the riverfront the courtyard pattern is regidly followed as a new factor in Shahjahan's architectural compositions. The Khas Mahal is the most stately royal residence with a facade of five cusped arches. In front of this palace lies Angoori Bagh- the quadripartite ornamental garden Angoori Bagh. A raised marble platform in the centre contains a small pool. The palace and the garden reinforce the paradisical imagery. Three large windows covered with elegant *jalis* provided views of the riverside scenery. Small niches in the hall contained paintings of the ruler's ancestore. The Khas Mahal and Angoori Bagh still have the haunting grandeur of stage after the performance. The dramatis personae have all left, leaving behind fleeting images of splendour, pomp and show: here were held the marriages of Dara Shikoh and Sultan Shuja when the palace gardens overflowed with beauties and dignitaries and reverberated with music and the rustle of silk.

The Khas Mahal is flanked by two small pavilions with bangla roofs covered with copper sheets. The bangla roofs, parapet and chhajja appear on structures specially related to the royal presence. Like the *Naulakha* pavilion in Lahore, these pavilions were used, in all likelihood for the *jharokha darshan*, king's ceremonial appearance before his loving subjects assembled beyond the ramparts below.

Musamman Burj, north of Khas Mahal, is the most ornate pavilion built by Shahjahan, replacing the original work of Jehangir. The central octagonal room has a verandah of slender Shahjahan columns overlooking the spectacular Yamuna negotiating a sharp eastward bend. An open hall with an ornamental fountain stands on the western side of the pavilion. This whole pavilion is covered with most charming ornamentation in *pietra dura*. The walls are covered with *chinikhana* (ornamental small niches for displaying vases and bottles), and floral motifs carved in relief on the dados. It is from the octagonal riverside verandah that Shahjahan gazed at the Taj Mahal, the tomb of his beloved queen Mumtaz, during the last years of his incarceration imposed by Aurangzeb. Here Shahjahan breathed his last. A small copper-coverd octagonal chhattri crowns Musamman Burj, the private apartments of Shahjahan which, from the ramparts below, looks the quintessence of romantic charm: "a casement high and triple-arch'd there was / All garlanded with carven imaag 'ries", as envisioned by John Keats, the English Romantic poet.

The Macchi Bhawan is a large courtyard surrounded by single and double-storeyed arcades. On the southern side is the projecting canopy with four baluster columns supporting curved roof, plain rounded arches and a sun medallion carved on the top. The subterranean chambers around the Macchi Bhawan housed the *harem* and the treasury. A gateway on the eastern section leads to the market, exclusive to the use of royal women- the place where Shahjahan first met Arjumand Banu, the future lady of the Taj.

Diwan-i-Khas, positioned between Musamman Burj and Macchi Bhawan, stands on the terrace. It is a very important palace used for extremely confidential conferences between the ruler and his ministers. It has a five cusped arches on the facade overlooking the terrace and three arches opening toward the east and western sides. The decoration is rich in *pietra dura* work on the marble columns. The inner section is covered with miniature arches and flowers carved in relief. There are two marble seats on the terrace. The one in black marble was used by Jehangir as the rebel prince at Allahabad, brought here after his coronation.

The two small mosques Mina Masjid and Nagina Masjid, are the private royal chapels. The Nagina Masjid has baluster columns, curved parapet and chhajja. Both completed in 1637 stand surrounded by royal palaces.

Moti Masjid, completed in 1653, after Shahjahan had moved to Delhi, is the most elegant of Shahjahan's mosques. Built entirely in white marble with three bulbous domes and chattris, the mosque has no ornamentation on its triple-aisled and seven-bayed interior. The courtyard is surrounded by arcaded galleries with three entrance portals approached by a flight of steps. Moti Masjid has no Quranic inscriptions, Inscriptions on this mosque are in praise of Shahjahan. The architectural grandeur of the Moti Masjid depends much on the intrinsic splendour of the marble itself.

Shahjahan extended his patronage to the Jami Masjid built by Jahanara, the princess. In 1648 she built here this mosque of excellent proportions in red sandstone. The arches are not cusped but of the conventional Tudor order. There are elegant small chattris on the parapet. The domes are heavy, without constricted necks or drum in the Persian tradition, but covered with a chevron pattern outlined in white marble. The general appearance of this large mosque is impressive.

Chini Ka Rauza is the octagonal tomb of Afzal Khan, Shahjahan's finance minister and brother of the famous calligraphist Amanat Khan. This is the only example of a tomb covered with decoration in glazed tiles in blue, green and yellow colours. The soffit of the dome is lined with concentric tiers of arched muqarnas and painted in extremely rich hues in the tradition of ornamentation on stucco during Jehangir's rule. The exterior of this tomb is much damaged but it is the solitary example of a tomb completely ornamented in tiles.

facing page. Bangla Pavilion, Agra Fort.

above. Glazed tile decoration at the Chini ka Rauza, Agra.

17

TAJ MAHAL & SHAHJAHANABAD

On June 17, 1631 Mumtaz Mahal died, after delivering her 14th child-Gauharara. She was given a temporary burial in Burhanpur. Her body was brought to Agra before the end of the year when the construction began on a tomb for the empress. The land had been purchased from Mirza Raja Jai Singh of Amber. Within six years the tomb was nearly complete while work on the subsidiary buildings continued for another six years, to be fully ready in 1643.

The Taj Mahal is only a part of an extensive architectural complex comprising caravan serais, residences for craftsmen and artisans, mosques and tombs, markets and other public utility buildings. The whole project required intensive planning in advance, leaving out nothing for a later-day addition. Engineers, mathematicians and architects pooled together their expertise to design what proved to be the most ambitious and magnificent architectural achievement of the Mughals, particularly Shahjahan the perfectionist, who personally looked into the minutest details of the project wherein as Peter Mundy's eyewitness account relates: "Gold and silver esteemed common Metall, and Marble but as ordinarie stones". Marble was procured from Makrana in Rajasthan and colourful precious and semi-precious stones for the ornamentation in *pietra dura* from different other countries. From the beginning of work at the tomb, the Taj was destined to become the most beautiful and splendid building in the world.

The Chauk-i-Jilau Khana, an immense arcaded courtyard, 268m long and 134m wide, with 128 rooms for attendants, is the first introduction to the Taj complex. On the northern side is the Sirhi Darwaza, a grand portal leading to Mumtazbad, now called Taj Ganj, the colony of stone cutters and master masons. Nearly 20,000 people worked at the Taj Mahal daily, till its completion in 1643.

A magnificent gateway in red sandstone provides entrance to the garden. It is a 30m high structure, massive and grand. The *pishtaq* set within a rectangular frame has floral arabesque in the spandrels and Quranic inscriptions on panels-the work of Abdul Haqq Shirazi, better known as Amanat Khan whose calligraphy decoration at the gateway to Akbar's tomb was much admired by Shahjahan. One of these inscriptions reads: "enter thou My Paradise", underlines the paradisical imagery which informs the whole architectural scheme at the Taj. Twenty six chattris, big and small, built over the parapet contribute charm to this gateway which is an independent architectural achievement in its own

right. There is nothing less than perfect at the Taj Mahal.

The first view of the Taj Mahal framed within the arch in the dark interior of the gateway, is most stunning and an unforgettable experience of life. As George Michell observes, it is "an ingenious perspective carefully devised for maximum architectural impact". The white marble tomb stands across the garden. So distant and alluring.

The garden at the Taj follows the duadripartite arrangement. Four stately water channels issue from the spectacular marble platform in the centre which bulbous dome. At the culmination of canals on the east and west sides, stand two identical, double-storeyed pavilions. These pavilions are superb examples of garden architecture affording wonderful views of the dappled garden and the tomb beyond the vast stretch of greenery. Each of the four large sections of the garden is further sub-divided into four sections by paved pathways. The star-shaped pattern of the parterres along the canals is still preserved in its original form. The concept of the char bagh, initiated by Babur in India, appears in its most magnificent form at the Taj Mahal.

At the northern end of the garden, a slightly raised platform in red sandstone, provides ideal space for the building. Sharing this platform with the tomb structure at the centre are two identical structures of the mosque on the west and the jamat khana or guest house on the east. Both these structures have triple domes. The interior is richly poly-chromed. The arches are inlaid with marble panels and the dados have floral motifs carved in relief. At the far ends of these structures stand grand tiered multi-faceted pavilions, overlooking the river.

Between the two structures stands the 6.7m high and 95m square podium in white marble with imposing minarets at the four corners. These tapering minarets are 41.6m high topped by octagonal chattris. They have a slight tilt away from the main body of the tomb so that in case of a natural calamity like earthquake they do not collapse on the tomb. It is only a minor illustration of the engineering skill with which every small detail has been taken care of. These minarets are now an integral part of the funerary and mosque architecture but with varying positions. At Akbar's tomb the minarets appear on the top of the gateway. At Itmad-ud-daula, these minarets appear as small engaged towers over the main tomb. At Jehangir's tomb, the minarets appear at the corners of the podium. At the Taj Mahal, the white marble colour of the main fabric assimilates the minarets into the whole architectural conception. The podium is 95m square.

The architectural plan of the tomb follows the nine-fold (hasht-bihisht) pattern, originating in Timurid buildings in Persia and Central Asia, and finding its first full expression on Humayun's tomb where it was introduced by Mirak Mirza Ghiyas, from Herat. The Timurid origin of the lay-out appealed to Shahjahan who was proud of his Timurid heritage and himself adopted one of the titles of Timur-Sahib Kiran.

The tomb is a Baghdadi octagon, a square with chamfered corners. On all four sides appears a high pishtaq, flanked by double storeyed arched niches framed within rectangular bands of inscription of verses from the Quran. The entire text of the Chapter 36 of the Quran has been inscribed on these four pishtaqs. The calligraphy has been ingeniously fashioned and graduated in size. Letters over the top band are one and a quarter times larger than those on the sides to create the look of uniformity and see that increasing height does not adversely affect their readability. Calligraphy in Islam is a sacred art, directly linked to God. The dados are covered with floral motifs-tulips. Roses, lily and narcissus etc carved in relief. These are flowers of paradise which unconsciously drive the mind towards the Throne of God.

The majestic, swelling dome rises to a height of 56.9m crowned by a brass finial, 17.1m high. It stands surrounded by four chattris. The constricted neck of the dome raises it over the high pishtaq so that it does not stand obliterated from view, as noticed at buildings with a high pishtaq. The convex swell of the pearl-shaped dome is balanced by the concave recessed arches that cover the exterior of the tomb. The dome refracts light and the recesses absorb it creating patterns of light and shade, solids and voids.

The interior comprises eight rooms, surrounding the central octagonal chamber containing the cenotaphs of Mumtaz Mahal at the centre and of Shahjahan to its west, the only example of asymmetrical work at the Taj. These cenotaphs are enclosed within an octagonal jali screen, supreme example of moucharabya, elaborate lattice work. Originally the cenotaphs were enclosed by a gold rail encrusted with gems and pearls, rubies and diamonds. For fear of vandalism, the gold railing was replaced by the present one in marble, well worth its weight in gold for the exquisite craftsmanship, the pride of Indian art. The jali screen or mahzar-i-mushakkab as it was called, has been fashioned with the jeweller's art and patience. Large single slabs of marble have been used on each side of the octagonal screen.

The cenotaphs are covered with the most consummate examples of pietra dura ornamentation. The setting of tiny pieces of hard precious stones into the hollows on the marble requires an extremely unflawed and perfect technique. A single petal can contain as many as 35 different variations of carnelian to create the desired hue and brilliance. The stones used here include coral, jasper, onyx, agate, amethyst, lapis, malachite etc. The decoration mostly consists of floral motifs, inspired by European herbals-tulips, poppies, honeysuckle, lily, fuschias creating in stone images of the Garden of Eden. One of inscriptions on the cenotaph of Mumtaz reads: "And allow them,

facing page. Entrance gateway to the Taj Mahal, Agra.

left. Elevation and layout plan of the Taj Mahal.

below. Marble screen enclosing the cenotaphs at the Taj Mahal.

bottom. Cenotaphs of Mumtaz Mahal and Shahjahan in the Taj Mahal.

O Lord: to enter the Garden of Eden which Thou has promised unto them" (from the Day of Judgment in the Quran).

Architecturally, the main hall has double-storeyed arcades topped by the semi-circular vault which forms the inner shell of the double dome. The interior has an unrelieved whiteness. The human voice uttered under the vault echoes 22 times.

The actual sarcophagi of the empress and the emperor lie in the crypt below the replicas on the upper floor. These are without any enclosing jali screen. The ninety nine names of Allah are inscribed over the sarcophagus of Mumtaz. On Shahjahan's sarcophagus are inscribed these words: "The illustrious sepulchre and sacred resting place of His Most Exalted Majesty dignified as Razwan (the Guardian of Paradise) having his abode in Paradise, and his dwellings in the starry heaven, inhabitant of the regions of bliss, the second Lord of the Qiran (the conjunction of Venus and Jupiter, when both he and Timur were born), Shahjahan, the king valiant. May his tomb ever flourish, and may his abode be the heavens. He travelled from this transitory world to the world of eternity on the night of the 28th of the month of Rajab 1076 AH (1666)."

The Persian influence on the whole conception of the Taj Mahal has been over emphasised. In fact, the Taj Mahal is the natural culmination of various architectural features introduced into the fabric of Indian architecture at various stages of its evolution: the char bagh, podium and the double dome had already appeared at the tombs of Sikandar Lodi. Humayun and Abdul Rahim Khan-i-Khana in Delhi, albeit in a less than perfect form. The Taj Mahal, guided by the vision and genius of Shahjahan, was able to a combine diverse features into an immaculate conception. Such a vast architectural project was realised with fullest cooperation form a team of architects including Ustad Isa Khan Effendi from Shiraz and his pupil Ustad Ahmad Lahori. The dome was designed by Ismail Khan. Makramat Khan and Abdul Karim were part of the large team. Shahjahan personally looked into the minutest details of the project, accepting or rejecting the ideas on sheer merit. "In a very real sense", as Bamber Gascoign observes, "the only architects of the Taj are Shahjahan and the Mughal tradition".

In this massive architectural project there was no place for the Italian jeweller Geronimo Veroneo whose claims on the design of the Taj were advanced by Father Manrique in 1641. This Italian designer of necklaces and bracelets, if at all he was consulted, ran away to Surat in 1632 when the project had just begun taking shape. Veroneo was too scared at the projected estimate of expenditure running into an unimaginable figure. He

vanished from the scene, escaping the emperor's ire but causing much mirth and chuckles to the real architects. There are historians still clinging to this preposterous tale of Veroneo.

Various architectural components of the Taj Mahal refer to the paradisical imagery, through the choice of the Quranic verses, the garden and the floral motifs, and the great pearl-shaped dome. The Taj Mahal stands not at the centre of the garden but at the extreme northern end in a clear allusion to the Divine Throne on the Day of Judgment. The dome at the Taj imitates the Throne of God surmounted by a gigantic pearl dome supported on four pillars from which flow the rivers of grace. The pearl symbolises the eternal nature, source of all creation, prototype of all that is quintessentially feminine in nature, suited to the tomb of Mumtaz Mahal.

The dome also unites earth and heaven. The square is the material universe, the octagon represents the transition, and the dome the vault of heave. Infinity is symbolised by the crowning crescent. The keel arch, a refrain repeated all over the tomb, is the shape central to Islamic architecture. It appears on the pishtaq, entrance arches, niches, windows, and on the podium, durm and chattris in an ornamental form. Water plays a crucial role in this cosmological imagery. It creates reversibility-the Quran is conceived as the mirror image of a tablet in heaven; the tree of life grows upside down in the garden of paradise. The Taj stands reflected in the garden canals, central marble pool and the Yamuna. Curiously, the image of the inverted lotus motif at the apex of the dome, a singularly indigenous element of architectural importance, supports this basic conception. In fact, repeated reference to the Garden of Eden in all the inscriptions, choice of verses relating to the Day of Judgment and the Throne of God suggestively underline Shahjahan's role as a semi-divine ruler.

In 1648, Shahjahan moved to his new capital-Shahjahanabad. He had not married again after the death of Mumtaz. In 1657 started the scramble for the throne occasioned by his brief illness. Aurangzeb chased Dara Shikoh, Shahjahan's favourite son and prospective heir, all over northern India (mostly on the routes and regions trudged on by Humayun when chased out of India by Sher Shah in 1540), imprisoned him and finally beheaded him to proclaim himself emperor. Shahjahan was confined to the Agra fort, allowed restricted movement within areas close to the Musamman Burj from where he could view the Taj Mahal. He refused to part with the crown jewels. The grand Mughal was fed on meals unfit for his servants. Jahanara was his only child to look after him. His health deteriorated fast, suddenly worsening on January 31, 1666. He couldn't swallow a drop of sherbet.

Niccalao Manucci relates a tale. A faqir (mendicant hermit) in Bijapur had warned that the day Shahjahan's hands stopped smelling of apples, he would die. The words flashed on the mind weakened with misery and illness. He raised his hands and sniffed. A sigh escaped his dry lips. The time to leave had come. He cast his last glances at the Taj Mahal from his bed in the Musamman Burj. His tired eyelids closed on a shattered heart and this world. And so, he died on January 31, 1666. "Abu'l Muzaffar Shihab-al-Din Muhammad Sahib-i-Qiran-Sani, Shahjahan Padshah Ghazi son of Nur-al-Din Jahangir Padshah, son of Akbar Padshah, son of Humayun Padshah, son of Babur

Padshah, son of Umar Shaikh Mirza, son of Sultan Abu Sa'id, son of Sultan Muhammad Mirza, son of Mirza Shah, son of Amir Timur Sahib-i-Qiran".

Jahanara planned a funeral procession befitting the great ruler. The purse containing 20,000 gold and silver coins for showering over the bier was confiscated. She was herself a prisoner and could not order others. A small number of insignificant minials carried the dead body through a postern on the riverside ramparts below the Musamman Burj. Quietly, unceremoniously Shahjahan made his exit from the magnificent palaces and pavilions. In the early hours of the day, the body of Shahjahan was entered into the crypt of the Taj Mahal to join Mumtaz Mahal, never to part again. It is said Shahjahan's favourite elephant Khalqdad, sensing the tragedy, also died as the burial was in progress. With Shahjahan's burial at the Taj Mahal were also finished forever the plans of another Taj Mahal in black marble, a plan hinted at by Tavernier.

Despite the gloom that enveloped his personal life after the death of Mumtaz Mahal, Shahjahan pursued his architectural projects with a surprising zeal. As soon as the Taj Mahal neared completion, he laid the foundation of a new city-Shahjahanabad, in 1639. Akbar had moved away from Delhi severing his link with the Imperial Delhi to found his own fort city of Agra and later Sikri. Agra had become too crowded and also, it was too hot. Shahjahan shifted his capital to the new city admirably built around the grand fort in red sandstone, called the Red Fort. The Red Fort epitomised the power and glory of the Mughal empire and Shahjahan's determination to establish his identity.

The Red Fort in Delhi is built on nearly the same architectural design as the fort in Agra. Qala-i-Mubarak (the fortunate citadel) as it was originally called, the fort covers an area of 2.5 km, made in the shape of a bow, with the straight riverside forming the string.

Two magnificent gateway-Lahori Gate and Akbarabadi Gate provide access to the palaces within. These gates open towards the main thoroughfares of the capital. The Lohori Gate, chief entrance portal, leads into the Chatta Chowk, the covered market with 32 arched bays. Ali Mardan Khan's covered market in Peshawar inspired Shahjahan to have a similar market in his fort which James Fergusson calls "the noblest entrance known to belong to any existing palace". The long vaulted aisle measures nearly 80m with an octagonal open court in the centre. The Chatta Chowk leads to Naqqar Khana or drum house where royal musicians played at fixed hours and announced arrival of dignitaries. No one, except members of the royal household, was allowed to ride horses beyond this point. This elegant structure is a double-storeyed construction in red sandstone.

Many subsidiary structures were pulled down by the British to make way for their military purposes. Still, the most important royal palaces have been allowed to survive to indicate the original splendour of the fort under Shahjahan.

The Diwan-i-Aam, hall of public audience, is the first royal building within the fort. Built in red sandstone covered with white shell plaster and gilding, this magnificent hall was where Shahjahan held his court amid scenes of extravagant grandeur. The royal throne, Nashiman-zilli-Ilahi (seat of the Shadow of God) stands on the eastern wall. Raised on a high podium I white marble with elegant baluster columns and the sloping bangala roof, this canopy is covered with enchanting pietra dura ornamentation. The black panels depicting birds and the panel depicting Orpheus playing flute to lion and hare were imported from Florence. The background panels depicting floral motifs and smaller birds are of Indian origin. Shahjahan had visions of his extraordinary power and by planting the Orpheus panel at the top, he prompts comparison with the throne of Solomon, an ideal model for justice. The lower portion of the podium is covered with floral motifs carved in relief. The new vocabulary of Imperial ornamentation includes Indian, Persian and European elements in a synthesis of divergent styles. Both Bernier and Travernier have left vivid accounts of the splendours of the Mughal court.

The Diwan-i-Aam is a nine-bayed and triple-aisled hall with twelve-sided columns supporting cusped arches, a scene of immense magnificence for the sheer beauty of its architectural features. The river-side pavilions have been carefully planned with an eye on the exploitation of the picturesque scenery as background to the imperial residences.

At the extreme northern end stands the Shah Burj, the octagonal tower decorated with glass mosaics. Now much ruined and truncated, the Shah Burj resembles the Musamman Burj at Agra. On the southern face of the Burj toward the rampart is a marble pavilion with cusped arches baluster columns and a chhajja in the curved bangala fashion. Behind this ornamental facade lies a scalloped marble basin fed by the nifir-i-bihisht (canal of paradise) built by Ali Mardan Khan. This long canal originating at Sirhind was excavated by Firoz Shah Tughlaq and allowed to decay over the years. Ali Mardan Khan revived it, brought it to Delhi through the Kabuli Darwaza from where it ran through the length of Chandni Chowk and entered the fort by means of a clever engineering device at the Shah Burj running through all the royal apartments and gardens. It functioned as the life-line of water supply in the garden and the fountains.

The royal *hammam* has some elegant glass mosaics and pietra

facing page. The Taj Mahal, Agra.

right. Detail of surface ornamentation on the Taj Mahal.

dura decoration. The *hammam* functioned as the emperor's private apartment for confidential consultations with grandees of the court.

The Diwan-i-Khas is a splendid building a rectangular structure with marble piers supporting cusped arches. The exterior has a classic simplicity. The interior has an extremely rich and fabulous ornamentation. The original silver ceiling was removed in the 18th century, replaced by the present wooden ceiling. Shahjahan's world-famous Peacock Throne, showpiece of Mughal wealth and splendour, was kept here on the grand marble platform. The Peacock throne, studded with the most exquisite rubies, pearls, gems and diamonds and emeralds on bands of gold. According to Travernier this throne cost nearly 12,037,500 sterling when it was made in Agra a few years back. It was plundered by Nadir Shah in 1739, dismantled and its pieces shared by his chiefs. Nothing remains of this throne Shahjahan's proud possession, not even an authentic depiction in contemporary miniatures.

The Diwan-i-Khas, was Shahjahan's hall of private audience. Built within a rectangular square, this palace used to be covered all around by magnificent tents and awnings. Splendid Persian carpets and glorious curtains created pictures of unprecedented grandeur. The red curtain enclosing the Diwan-i-Khas kept it out of bounds for men excluded from the charmed circle of power. The canal of paradise ran through the palace, under the royal throne. One of the inscriptions below the ceiling reads: "*Agar Firdaus bar rue Zamin as to, Namin asto, hamin asto hamin ast*" (if there is a paradise on earth, this is it, this is it, this is it). The splendour, pomp and show underlined Shahjahan's status as a semi-divine king and these architectural symbols of the Quranic paradise. The pietra dura decorations on piers and elegant jali screens on the riverside contribute their own charm to Diwan-i-Khas.

The palaces on the riverside are not built in a group. Instead, they are separated by considerable unbuilt areas. The *Khwabgah*, private chambers of Shahjahan, is a set of three small apartments with a projecting engaged tower for the jharokha darshan, the ruler's ritual appearance before his subjects. At the centre is a jali screen carved in extraordinary excellence. The scales of Justice are carved in relief over the top of the jali. The ceiling has some exquisite designs painted in gold and other lustrous hues. Inscriptions on the rounded arch at the centre relate to the cost of construction and the year of completion-1648.

The Rang Mahal is the *zenana* palace with twelve-sided piers supporting cusped arches. The openings toward the river, originally covered with *jalis* have now been filled up with stone. The nine-fold plan of Rang Mahal provides ample space for the

enjoyment of ladies. Traces of glass mosaics can still be seen in the corner rooms. The piece de resistance at the Rang Mahal is the lotus carved out of a single slab of marble, a rare example when the ruler indulged his craftsmen to exhibit their art. The lotus is a superb piece of sculpture ornamented with gems and pearls. Under the soft ripples of water, the lotus appears intensely charming.

The canal of paradise, as drawn by Ali Mardan Khan, was the real source of charm and scene of much frolic. Bernier observes: "Nearly every chamber has its reservoir of running water at the door; on every side are gardens, delightful alleys, shady retreats, streams, fountains, grottoes, deep excavations that afford shelter from the sun by day, lofty divans and terraces on which to sleep coolly at night. Within the walls of this enchanting place, in fine, no oppressive or inconvenient heat is felt." An ornamental garden with fountains lies in front of the Rang Mahal, only a slightly altered version of the Khas Mahal in Agra.

The two gardens built towards the Shah Burj Hayat Baksh and Mahtab Bagh were laid out on the char bagh pattern. Now only two marble pavilions, called Sawan and Bhadon after the Hindu months of rainy season, have survived. Mahtab Bagh (Moon light garden) was completely destroyed. The Hayat Baksh (life giving) Bagh has survived for these

two identical pavilions. Each stands on a podium at the top of which is a chute from which water descends into the chael, cascading over a set of niches at the base of the structure. Water here, as everywhere else in these garden palaces, added grandeur of its own.

The Masjid-i-Jahanuma or the great Jami Masjid of Shahjahanabad was nearly the last architectural enterprise of Shahjahan. Built in 1656 on top of a rocky prominence, the Jami Masjid is the largest mosque in India. It follows the conventional pattern of an open courtyard with surrounding pillared cloisters. The 91m square courtyard is spectacular, approached by a majestic flight of steps on the east, north and south sides leading to stately gateways, reminiscent of the great mosques of the Tughlaq period and the Jami Masjid in Jaunpur. The appearance of structural elements from the indigenous architectural tradition of the Sultanate shows the influence of a great heritage and also that no architecture, howsoever, magnificent it be, can isolate itself entirely from its roots in the soil.

The twelve sided chhattris at the four corners of the courtyard are splendid. The rectangular prayer hall is 61m by 27.5m with a façade of 11 cusped arches. The façade is decorated with marble panels carrying inscriptions regarding the construction of the mosque. The *pishtaq* rising high over the arches on both sides, has slender pinnacles at both ends. Three

magnificent bulbous domes, decorated with stripes in black marble rise over the sanctuary. The facade is flanked by two tall, 39.6m high, tapering minarets topped by chhattris. 130 spiral steps lead to the top of the minarets affording a breathtaking view of Shahjahanabad. The minarets are also decorated with stripes. Holy relics of the Prophet Muhammad a hair from his beard, an imprint of his foot on stone and some early copies of the Quran are kept in a wooden enclosure. These are Shahjahan's gift to this great congregational mosque.

above and right. Jami Masjid, Delhi.

147

Tomb of Rabia Daurani, wife of Aurangzeb. Aurangabad.

18

AURANGZEB
THE DECLINE OF
A GREAT TRADITION

The prolific and continued architectural activity, which characterises the rule of Shahjahan, exhausted itself with the beginning of Aurangzeb's rule. Aurangzeb remained preoccupied with designs of territorial aggrandizement in the southern part of India. Despite his known Islamic zeal, the number of mosques built under his patronage is too small. In fact, architectural activity did not interest him much. Quite predictably, dwindling patronage produced little work of any remarkable beauty. The steady decline of Mughal power during the last three decades of the 17th century was accompanied by an equally manifest degeneration of the great Mughal architectural tradition. Inspired patronage and vision-fountainhead of all great art, nearly dried up leaving behind uninspired, lack-lustre architectural creations.

The tomb of Rabia Daurani is the last monumental mausoleum of the great Mughal dynasty.

Raushan Ara, Aurangzeb's sister, chose to be buried in an open grave in a *hasht-bihisht* pavilion in the garden she had built for herself in Delhi. Jahanara Begum, Shahjahan's favourite daughter, also chose a still more modest burial in a grave at the dargah of Nizamuddin under a marble tablet with a touching inscription. "Let naught cover my grave save the green grass: for grass well suffices as a covering for the grave of the lowly". The only other contemporary sepulchral structure of some elegance is the tomb complex of Abd Allah Khan at Ajmer. This is a square structure with a domed hall over the tombstone. The multi-lobed arches and columns in marble betray their link with the architectural tradition fostered by Shahjahan who also built four elegant marble pavilions on Ana Sagar in Ajmer.

The Moti Masjid, the royal chapel built in 1662, continues the architectural standard achieved during the previous rule. This small triple-domed mosque copies the style of Shahjahan's Nagina Masjid in the fort at Agra. Here, the decorative quality of the structure has received greater attention. The inner side of the eastern wall is covered with relief carvings of domes, baluster columns and foliate forms. Architectural elements are turned into surface ornament. The contour of the domes, profusion of pinnacles and shape of finials suffers from over-emphasis. The interior is extremely ornate. The exuberant floral relief work on marble adds a sensuousness to the architecture which does not quite match the patron's professed austerity; yet another evidence of Aurangzeb's lack of involvement in the actual implementation of architectural undertakings during his rule, giving greater freedom to artisans leading to unpremeditated results.

The tomb of Rabia Daurani, Aurangzeb's wife, was built in 1660-61. It was designed by Ata Ullah, son of Ustad Ahmad who worked at the Taj Mahal. This tomb in Aurangabad is a soulless copy of the great original in Agra. The garden, domes and minarets follow the outlines of the Taj but here the building is completely bereft of any elegance and, as James Fergusson observes, "narrowly escapes vulgarity and bad taste". The scale is much smaller and the whole structure looks rather compressed. The dome surrounded by cupolas demands more space. The alteration in the form of the octagonal structure appears as square pilasters at the quoins in place of chamfered angles creating an accentuated verticality at the cost of a well-proportioned and harmonious unity of structural parts. The upper storey looks over crowded with the dome, chhattris and pinnacles jostling for space. The floral motifs borrowed from the marble edifices of Shahjahan begin to show a certain stiffness.

The prayer hall of the Moti Masjid is inlaid with outlines of musallas (small carpets for prayers) in black marble. It stands at a high platform on the western part of the courtyard enclosed by high walls for strict privacy. The three bulbous domes, originally copper-plated, appear too constricted at the neck. The parapet below the central dome, curved in the typical bangala style, has been decorated with a thin band of floral motifs in *pietra dura*. The Moti Masjid is a structure of the most refined and polished standard generally identified with Shahjahan rather than Aurangzeb. The exaggeration of certain architectural elements clearly shows that the best work belongs to the past. Decline has set in.

The Badshahi Masjid in Lahore (1674) is built in the familiar Mughal tradition-red sandstone and white marble. It is the largest mosque of the Mughal kingdom, elevated on a high platform and a grand, double-storeyed gateway. High tapering minarets mark the corners of the majestic courtyard while octagonal turrets with chattris fráme the prayer hall. The three bulbous domes in white marble rise over cylindrical drums constricted at the neck. The interior has been lavishly decorated with elaborate relief work in painted plaster. The five arched openings on each side of the central arch are rather small in size in relation to the massive scale of the building, creating that spatial tension now identified with Aurangzeb's architecture by Catherine Asher. The mosque, a massive structure executed in the finest architectural tradition, lacks the impact of a guiding spirit which alone raises the ordinary to an extraordinary level.

The mosque at Mathura bears a close resemblance to the Badshahi Masjid. All entrances are cusped and there is little ornamentation with inlaid marble work. The free-standing pavilions with bangala roofs show a predilection towards ornamental features characteristic of the preceding era. Ornateness of decoration and structural elements like bangala roof and baluster columns associated with the emperor's semi-divine character and appearing on royal thrones during Shahjahan's rule now comes to be associated with religious architecture under Aurangzeb.

Unlike his predecessors Jehangir and Shahjahan, Aurangzeb showed no interest in constructing gardens, restricting visits to Kashmir by royalty and nobles only after royal permission. The only garden attributed to him is at Fatehabad, near Agra. It was built to celebrate his victory over his brothers in the battle of succession in 1659. The large rectangular pavilion in red sandstone and bricks resembles the Rang Mahal at the Fort in Delhi. The other garden at Pinjore, near Chandigarh, was built by Fidai Khan Koka. It is a splendid terraced garden exploiting natural mountain springs. The pavilions have cusped arches on baluster columns. This garden recreates the splendour of the Shalamar and Nishat gardens in Srinagar.

After a protracted stay in the southern India, Aurangzeb died in 1707. He was buried in an open grave at Khuldabad, near the Ellora caves. The Imperial capital, following the death of the last great Mughal emperor, witnessed an unseemly struggle for the crown adversely affecting all architectural activity which now was limited to small tombs and inconspicuous mosques. Zinat-al-Nisa, Aurangzeb's second daughter, built a mosque on a high plinth in 1711. The seven-arched facade is surmounted with three domes decorated with alternating stripes in red and white marble and flanked by minarets carrying similar decoration following the pattern of decoration at Shahjahan's Jami Masjid. The mosque, tomb and madarsa of Ghaziu'd-Din Khan, an influential courtier during the rule of Aurangzeb was built before his death in 1709 near Ajmeri Gate. The gateway is very impressive and the mosque is distinguished for its three large bulbous domes. Originally covered with stripes of red and black stone, now whitewashed. His open-air grave lies enclosed within walls of *jali* screens. The madarsa has been a seat of high learning in the capital for over 300 years.

Aurangzeb's death in 1707 precipitated the degeneration of the Mughal power. His successors were mere pale shadows of the Imperial dignity and power, playing as mere puppets in the hands of scheming nobles and pawns to factionalism. The sack of Delhi by Nadir Shah from Persia in 1739 destroyed any semblance of authority. Delhi was plundered. Nadir Shah carried with him Shahjahan's Peacock Throne and the Kohinoor diamond, and also thousands of craftsmen besides unimaginable treasure. Before this destruction and plunder was forgotten, there appeared in Delhi another brigand from Afghanistan Ahmad Shah Abdali. He visited Delhi five times, leaving behind scenes of destruction and misery. Muhammad shah, king of Delhi, was a pathetic figurehead who died in 1748. It was unmitigated misery thereafter, a story that ran unchanged for another 100 years.

facing page. Moti Masjid, built by Auragzeb, Red Fort, Delhi.

right. Pinjore Garden built by Fidai Khan, near Chandigarh, Punjab.

Ahmad Shah, who succeeded Muhammad Shah, was a dissolute ruler. The only contribution he made to Delhi's architectural heritage is limited to the Qudsia Bagh he built for his mother in the 1750s. An idea of the ruler's poverty and helplessness can be had from the fact that the only structure of some importance was built courtesy Nawab Shujauddaula of Awadh (Lucknow) for his father Mirza Muqim Abdul Mansur Khan, titled Safdarjang, viceroy of Awadh under Muhammad Shah and later on prime minister under Ahmad Shah. The tomb, built in 1753, was to be the last building in the great Mughal tradition of architecture. The model chosen for the structure is Humayun's tomb and the material obtained from the tomb of Abdul Rahim Khan-i-Khana.

The tomb of Safdarjang or the madarsa, as it is called, is built within an enclosed Char Bagh. It is a double-storeyed structure over an arcaded terrace, 30m side and 3m high. The large central arched alcove is flanked by smaller alcoves. The four engaged turrets with chhattris at the corners, a large, almost spherical dome, and lavish ornamentation on the exterior-chief architectural dome, and a lavish ornamentation on the exterior-chief architectural elements of this tomb have been used to emphasize the verticality of the structure. The arches and the dome look impressive. The garden is well-planned. If Safdarjung still suffers in comparison with the more famous examples in this tradition-tombs of Humayun, Akbar, Shahjahan and Mumtaz, the reason is not far to seek. The whole Mughal empire in the 1750s was in utter doldrums. Despite the depleted power and treasury, the tomb of Safdarjung is an impressive monument, no mean triumph of art over adverse and instable political circumstances.

The rule of the Mughal dynasty continued limpingly till 1858 when the British finally got rid of Bahadur Shah II and banished him to Rangoon bringing to an unceremonious end the rule of Babur established in 1526. The only two small structures ascribed to Bahadur Shah II are the red sandstone pavilion in the Hayat Bakash Bagh in the Red Fort and a small palace, called Zafar Mahal, near the dargah of Bakhtiyar Kaki in Mehrauli.

The disintegration of the Mughal power had already set in with the rise to power of principalities in Awadh (Lucknow), Murshidabad, and in southern India. These new independent rulers only tried to emulate the splendour of Mughal architecture in their own creations. Their limited resources and singular want of creative imagination led them to adopt a florid ornamental mode, over-emphasised bulbous dome and shapes, and an increasing reliance on stuccowork. It was to Shahjahan's architecture rather than to the buildings of Akbar that they turned for inspiration-multi-lobed arches, bangala roofs, baluster columns, engaged corner shafts etc. used on mosques and tombs, pavilions and palaces.

The Nawabs of Faizabad, later on of Lucknow, were Khurasani Persians. They were aesthetically inclined prolific builders and great patrons of fine arts. Muhammad Shah had appointed Saadat Khan Burhan-ul-Milk as the first Subehdar of Awadh as early as 1724 whose successors held immense power and wealth during the following century.

The Lucknow Nawabs were the rallying force for Shiism in this part of the country. Besides palaces and mosques they built Imambadas used for Shia celebrations of Muharram and storing Tazias. The Bada Imambada, built by Asaf-ud-Daula in 1784 as a famine relief work, is one of the most impressive buildings in Lucknow. This vast architectural complex has massive gateways, a large mosque, spectacular courtyards and the Imambada at the western end of the complex. The large single-storeyed vaulted hall has an immense interior, 49m by 16m. The height of the simple but tremendous vault is 15m. It is one of the largest vaulted halls of its kind. The decorative treatment looks rather poor. A long line of domed chhattris stands over the parapet to provide a conspicuous feature of ornamentation on the exterior.

The architectural features of the mosque comprise familiar elements but further distinguished by a distinct sense of spaciousness. The details of construction disappoint on closer inspection. The shape of the domes with their foliated fluting is

facing page. Tomb of Safdarjung, Delhi.

below. Bada Imambada, Lucknow.

Bibi ka Maqbara at Aurangabad and the Taj at Husainabad Imambada in Lucknow show how far away the artisans have moved from that original Mughal memorial of love. Art, once past its peak and prime, fails to repeat itself.

Work on the Jami Masjid was begun during the rule of Muhammad Shah. It is an elegant structure with three domes and lofty minarets. The mosque retains some feature of the Mughal style. Though its ornate exterior suffers from excessive elaboration, resembling the mosque at the Qudsia Bagh in Delhi, it is one of the better examples of architecture in Lucknow. Other examples of architecture during the twilight of the Nawabi rule in Lucknow include Qaiser Bagh palaces of Wazid Ali Shah (1848-1850) the last Nawab of Lucknow. These sprawling palaces are known for their decadent style and florid ornamentation on stucco. It was intended to be larger than Tuileries and Louvre combined but its size alone cannot defend its incoherence and jumble of hybrid Indo-European facades.

The buildings in Lucknow are far too many to discuss but all characterised by the decadent spirit pervading the seat of pleasure-seeking Nawabs. Constantia (the present La Martiniere Boys' School) was built by Maj. General Claude Martine (1735-1800) political agent working as intermediary between the Nawabs and the British Resident. The debased Palladian style of this immense chateau has drawn much attention. It is built on a high podium, comprising a massive symmetrical block with curved semi-circular wings. Corner pavilions, statuary posted on high points, stately staircase, heraldic lions are all assembled here to form a meaningless architectural medley of the most interesting king. Constantia was the first large building of the mixed European order, distinguished for symbolising the introduction of European elements in Indian architecture coinciding with the complete degeneration of the classic Mughal tradition.

Srirangapatnam, near Mysore, was the seat of two well known Mysore Sultans Haider Ali (1760-82) and Tipu Sultan (1782-99). The Darya Daulat palace has elegant proportions and lavish decoration in gorgeous colours, mostly battle scenes. The Gumbad-i-Ala or the tombs of both father and son, is built in the architectural style of Bijapur. The square structure is of a large size, surmounted by a graceful dome and minarets. The tomb structure is enclosed by a verandah.

The Jami Masjid is distinguished for its grand octagonal minarets containing stairs and pierced by holes for admitting light and air. These picturesque minarets are crowned with turnip-shaped masonry domes. The projecting balconies at every stage provide panoramic views of the island fort.

Murshidabad, in Bengal, contains some fine examples of architecture in the 18th century. The Katra Masjid (1724-25) was completed before the death of Nawab Murshid Quli Khan. The inspiration for the structure, particularly the four corner octagonal minarets, is derived form the Badshahi Masjid of Aurangzeb in Lahore. The Chowk Masjid (1767), built by Munni Bai, widow of the Nawab Mir Jafar, is a large building with seven bays and five graduated domes. It is covered with rich ornamentation in stucco. Murshidabad has many other mosques

uninspiring and the whole structure betrays a slackening in vitality.

The Rumi Darwaza, gateway to the imambada complex of building is one of the magnificent gateways of its class. The ornamentation over the arched entrance is in the style typical of architecture at Lucknow. Percy Brown calls Rumi Darwaza "a meretricious and fantastic creation, the whole in dubious taste". Surely it lacks the grandeur of classic outlines and proportions of the Buland Darwaza at Sikri or the gateway to Akbar's tomb at Sikandara. The Rumi Darwaza reflects the taste of the Nawabs, but so far away from Delhi and Agra, this gateway has an unmistakable elegance, characteristic of architecture during the phase of decadence. Catherine Asher defends the work at Rumi Darwaza as "highly creative, characterised by a sense of dynamic articulation never expressed in the more orderly structures of the Mughals".

The Musainabad Imambada, built by Muhammad Ali Shah in 1837 has according to George Michell a "fairy-tale appearance". Standing over an ornamental tank full of lotus and small fish, this small ornamental structure is flanked by a copy of the Taj and a mosque. The whole structure whole surely shock the purists for the tawdriness and florid quality of ornamentation. It surely illustrates the limits of imitations and the degeneration of form caused by such an effort. The two imitation of the Taj Mahal the

and tombs with no architectural pretension, showing an aged tradition advancing towards the inevitable end without a whimper.

The use of Tuscan columns at the Imambada (1847) and the grand European facade of the Aina Mahal or the Nawab's palace designed by General Duncan Macleod in 1837 mark the introduction of European architectural elements into the fabric of India architecture which still persisted with features popularised by the great Mughal builders not so long ago.

Mughal architecture shows a creative comingling of Timurid or Persian architectural elements with the ornamental sandstone tradition of the architecture of the Delhi Sultanate. In due course, the strong characteristic features of the Gujarat, Malwa, Rajasthan architecture assumed greater influence, particularly during the rule of Akbar in the 16th century. The palaces at Fatehpur Sikri bear testimony to the influence of traditional Indian architecture on the Muslim architecture in northern India. The irregular layouts of forts and palaces built by Akbar is characteristic of this period, emanating, in no small degree, from their still persisting Mughal inclination towards the layouts of their tent encampments during long journeys across the country on hunting and military campaigns. Gardens, tombs and mosques self-contained structural units, followed rigid geometrically correct layout plans. The nine-fold (hasht-bihisht) plan, regular and irregular octagon, and a square or rectangular block surrounded by an ambulatory verandah based on the Gujarati models remained the most frequently used forms of architecture. The Delhi Sultanate tradition or the Lodi style square tomb was never entirely forgotten, being used on smaller structures at regular intervals. The use of red sandstone ornamented with white marble lining on the elevation remained a constant feature of exterior decoration. Akbar's architecture symbolises the first full climax of the great Mughal architectural tradition in India.

Jehangir and Shahjahan ushered in the Age of Marble. Complete structures were built in marble reducing red sandstone to a secondary status. The *pietra dura* ornamentation reached unprecedented perfection and splendour. Architectural forms during this period assumed a definite sensuous appearance, in place of the masculine and vigorous appearance of Akbari buildings. The Taj Mahal symbolised not only eternal love but also brought to a culmination the best features of Indian architecture, albeit a distinctive Persian flavour which only enhanced its splendour.

Almost all-prominent tombs are built on a high podium. A bulbous double-dome in marble crowns octagonal structures with chamfered corners (Baghdadi octagon). Minarets form an integral part of the architectural scheme at mosque and tombs, their placement revised constantly to suit the layout plan of the building.

The gardens form an important part of the Mughal

facing page, left. Mosque at Bada Imambada, Lucknow.

below. Rumi Darwaza, Lucknow.

following pages. Chota Imambada, Lucknow.

contribution to Indian architecture. Gardens on the river front and on the hillsides introduced a very popular architectural form the *baradari*, an open pillared pavilion set amidst fountains and water channels. The Char Bagh or the four-fold layout of the garden around tombs of Humayun, Akbar, Shahjahan and Mumtaz Mahal are among the greatest and aesthetically most pleasing Indian gardens, inspiring numerous imitations in the provincial capitals. The emphasis on geometrically correct layouts and bilateral symmetrical planning characterise architecture of Shahjahan in the second phase, yet another peak of classical splendour inspired by Persian architecture and adaptation of indigenous architectural forms-curvilinear bangala, thatched roof form Bengal.

Away from the Imperial capital, the architectural forms in provinces remained inclined towards ornamentation on stucco, creating a superficial resemblance to classical Mughal forms in domes and pinnacles, nearly over-doing it as seen at Aurangabad and Lucknow. Nearly all provincial architecture built after the Akbar-Shahjahan period tended to suffer from an overdose of 'Mughalisation', as Ebba Koch points put, The bulbous dome, multi lobed arches, baluster columns, glass mosaics and stucco work-identified with the glorious Mughal architecture, came to form a permanent part of the local architectural idiom in distant corners of the country, a spell eventually broken by the introduction of European feature towards the end of the 19th century. It is with this Europeanisation of Indian architecture that the long reign of Mughal architecture comes to an end. Every city and village has its mosque and tombs. Important cities have their own 'Delhi Gate'. Long after the Mughal and the Nawabs left the scene the influence of their architectural glory lingers on, appearing in numerous versions.

below. La Martiniere, Lucknow.

facing page. Replica of the Taj Mahal at the Chota Imambada, Lucknow.

GLOSSARY

Abacus
flat slab above the capital on a column

Acanthus
a variety of plant with fleshy leaves, generally appears in Greek Art

Aisle
lateral divisions on both sides of the nave

Alcove
a vaulted recess in a wall

Arabesque
typical Islamic ornament, intertwining of floral and geometrical forms

Arcade
range of arches raised on piers orcolumns

Architrave
part of an entabulature, comprising the beam over two or more columns; moulded frame to a door or window

Arcuate
building style using arches in place of beams

Ashlar
hewn blocks of masonry

Bagh
garden

Baldachin
canopy or covering over a throne or staue

Baluster
cypress bodied column with a tapering shaft forming a bulb at the root

Barrel-vault
cylindrical form of roof or ceiling

Baoli
underground stepwell

Baradari
rectangular/square pavilion with 12 pillars

Bangla/Bangaldar
curved roof or vault with eaves curved on both axes as on the huts in Bengal
Bas relief
low-projection carving

Batter
slope on the wall

Bay
a compartment between pillars

Beam
a wooden or stone lintel

Bracket
projecting support, below a lintel or eave

Burj
tower

Buttress
support built against a wall

Caravanserai
public inn for merchants and travellers; generally a large enclosure with one or two gates, single or double-storeyed arrangement of rooms with facilities. Large caravanserais include mosque, market and bath etc.

Chadar
sloping chute for water channels and ornamental effect

Chajja
overhanging eave or dripstone to protect from rain or sun

Char bagh/Chahr Bagh
four-fold garden; the Mughal form of char bagh had the square plan divided into four quarters by paved pathways (khiyabans) and water courses

Chattri
a small domed kiosk, open-pillared construction

Chihil-sutun
forty pillared hall; (numerous pillars, number not exactly forty)

Chini khana
wall with panels of small niches for placing vases and bottles; also a decorative motif

Clerestory
upper portion of wall pierced by windows

Corbel
blocks of stone projecting from the wall

Crenellate
battlements or loopholes

Cusp
projecting points between small arcs of an archway

Dargah
shrine complex of a Muslim saint

Daulat Khana-i-Khass
Hall of Private Audience, the term introduced by Shahjahan, earlier called ghusl khana

Daulat Khana Khasso-Aam
Hall of public audience, hypostyle construction

Double-dome
dome with an outer and an inner shell of masonry

Drum
base of the drum, circular or octagonal

Embrasure
splayed opening in wall or fortification

Enciente
enclosure

Engrailed
foliated, cusped

Faience
earthenware, porcelain

Fenestration
window or openings

Flange
projecting flat rim, collar, rib

Foliated
carved with leaf ornament

Gumbad
dome or domed tomb

Hammam
bath, bathhouse with separate rooms for hot

and cold water and changing rooms; Turkish bath

Hadith
traditions related to the life of the Prophet

Hauz
pool, tank

Hisht bihisht
eight paradises; building on a nine-fold plane, "a square or a rectangle, often with chamfered corner so as to form an irregular octagon, is divided by four intersecting construction lines into nine parts; a central domed chamber, rectangular open halls in the middle of the sides (in the form of either a pishtaq or a Mughal Iwan) and double-storey vaulted corner rooms (blocks). There is no hard evidence that this term, which has been coined for Timurid architecture, was actually current in Mughal India". Ebba Koch

Hijra
622, year of Muhammad's flight from Mecca from which the Muslim calender is dated

Hypostyle
hall with ceiling supported on columns, not walls

Idgah
open air place of prayer (namaz) and Muslim congregations

Imambada
tomb of a shi'ite holy man

Impost
architectural member on which the arch immediately rests

Intarsia
mosaic of tinted or natural wood

Intrados
inner curve of an arch

Iwan
Large recessed arch on entrance; single vaulted hall, walled on three sides and opening directly to the outside of the fourth

Jali
perforated screen with ornamental design on

wood or stone

Jami Masjid
congregational mosque, Friday mosque

Jharokha
overhanging oriel window, supported on brackets

Jihad
holy war against non-believers, striving in the way of God
Keystone
central stone of an arch

Khanqah
residence for sufis

Khiyaban
paved (raised) pathway

Khwabgah
sleeping apartment

Lat
column

Liwan
hall for prayer, covered part of a mosque

Loggia
an open-to-the-air gallery, verandah

Machicolations
projecting parapet carried on brackets

Madarsa
school for religious instruction

Maqsura
screen or arched facade of a mosque

Merlon
parapet battlements with pointed tops

Mihrab
arched niche in the qibla wall of a mosque, indicating the direction of Mecca to be faced for prayer

Mimbar
pulpit in a mosque, with steps

*Munabbatkar*i
relief work

Muqarnas
moulding with a web of miniature vaults, concave element in vaults

Naqqar khana
drum house

Nashiman
pavilion, seat

Nave
the central or main compartment; in a mosque it is the area in front of the central mihrab

Opus sectile
marble inlay of various colours

Parchin kari
stone intarsia

Pendentive
triangular surface by which a dome is supported over a square compartment

'Phase of transition'
structural system for converting the square into the base for a drum

Pietra dura
inlaid mosaic of hard and expensive stones

Pilaster
square pillar projecting from the wall

Pishtaq
high portal, gateway, monumental arched niche, usually half-domed, enclosed by a rectangular frame. The longer vertical sides are accentuated by engaged polygonal shafts terminating above the parapet in freestanding ornamental pinnacles or guldastas.

Pylon
tall, monumental gateway

Riwaq
cloister bordering the courtyard

Qibla
direction of prayer

Quoin
corner of a building

Qutb
axis, pivot

Rauza
cloister bordering the courtyard

Shahjahani column
multi-faceted column, a multi-faceted or muqarnas capital and a base in the form of an inverted cushion capital, whose four flat faces are given a cusped-arch outline recalling a stylized flower

Seraglio
walled palace

Sheesh Mahal
palace with glass-mosaic decoration

Spandrel
triangular space between the curve of an arch and the square enclosing it

Squinch arch
arched vault across the corner, built to support the dome rising over it

Stylobate
a platform on which stands a colonnade

Trabeate
beam-and-lintel construction

Transept
cross or transverse compartments of a building

Triforium
gallery or arcade above the arches of the nave

Turret
small tower, chiefly ornamental

Tympanum
an area enclosed by the pediment or arch; triangular space within the cornices of a pediment

Voussoir
one of a series of wedge-shaped stone forming an arch

Ziarat
holy Muslim tomb

BIBLIOGRAPHY

Ali, A.A., Memoirs of Gaur and Pandua, rev.ed.Calcutta, 1931

Ansari, M.A., European Travellers under the Mughals (1580-1627), rpt.Delhi, 1975 'Palaces and Gardens of the Mughals'. Islamic Culture. 1959

Asher, Catherine., Architecture of Mughal India, Cambridge, 1992 Islamic Monuments of Eastern India

Basham, A.L.(ed) A Cultural History of India, New Delhi, 1975

Basham, A.L., The Wonder that was India, New Delhi, 1981

Begley, W.E.and Desai, Z.A., Taj Mahal: The Illumined Tomb: An Anthology of Seventeenth Century Mughal and European Documentary Sources, Cambridge, Mass., 1989

Begley,W.E., 'The Myth of the Taj Mahal and a New Theory of its Symbolic Meaning', The Art Bulletin, 61

Bernier, F.,Travels in the Mughal Empire, 1656-1668, London, 1934

Beveridge, A.S. (trans.) The Baburnama, in English, 2 vols., London 1921, rept.New Dellhi 1970

Beveridge, H.(trans.) The Akbarnama of Abu-l-Fazl, 3 vols., Calcutta, 1970-1921(ed.) Jehangir's Tuzuk, Eng. Trans. by A. Rogers , 2 vols, 1909-14 rept Delhi 1968

Blair, Sheila S. and Bloom, J.M., The Art and Architecture of Islam, Ahmedabad, 1995

Blochman, M., and Jarrett (trans.) The Ain-i-Akbari by Abul Fazl Allami, 3 vols. Calcutta, 1873-94

Brand, Micharel and Dowry. G.D. (eds) Fatehpur Sikri, Marg, Bombay, 1987 Akbar's India: Art from the Mughal. City of Victory, N.Y. 1985

Brend, Barbara., Islamic Art, London, 1999

Brown, Percy., India Architecture: Islamic Period, Delhi, 1942

Burgess, J., The Mohammedan Architecture of Ahmedabad, A.S.I. of West India,
        Vol. VII, 1900
Burgess, J. and Cousens, H., Mohammedan Architecture in Gujarat,
        London,1929
Burgess, J.Antiquities in Bidar and Aurangabad Districts, Arch.sur. of West India, Vol.III, 1878

Chaghtai, M.A., 'Pietra-Dura Decoration of the Taj', Islamic Culture, 15, 1941

Chandivala, B.K., Dilli ek Khog, Delhi, 1964

Chenoy, S.M., Shahjahanabad: A City of Delhi 1638-1857. Delhi, 1998

Chopra, P., Delhi: History and Places of Interest, Delhi

Cole, H.H., Architecture of Ancient Delhi: Especially the Buildings Around the Kutb Minar, London, 1975

Cousens, H., Bijapur and its architectural Remains, Arch.Sur. of India, vol.xxxvii, Imp.Sur. of India, Bombay, 1916

Crane, Howard., 'The Patronage of Zahir al-Din Babur and the Origin of Mughal Architecture', Bulletin of the Asia Institute, NSI, 1987

Craven, R.c., Indian Art, London, 1976

Crowe, S., The Gardens of Mughal India, London, 1972

Daniel, Thomas and William., Oriental Scenery, London, 1795-1805

Dayal, Maheshwar., Rediscovering Delhi: the Story of Shahjahanabad, Delhi, 1975

Davies, Philips., Monuments of India, the Penguin guide., vol.II (Islamic, Rajput and European), London, 1989

Desai, Z.A., Indo Islamic Architecture, New Delhi, 1970

Dowson, Elliot and John. (eds.) The History of India as told by its Historians, 8 vols., London, 1869

Eaton, Richard M., Essays on Islam and Indian History, Oxford, 2000

Eden, Emily., Up the Country, London 1937

Fanshawe, H.C., Delhi: Past and Present, London, 1902

Fass, Virginia., The Forts of India, London, 1986

Fasihuddin, M., The sharqi Monuments of Jaunpur, Allahabad, 1922

Fergusson, J., History of Indian and Eastern Architecture, London, 1899

Finley, E.B., Nur Jahan: Empress of Mughal India Oxford. 1993

Forrest, G.W., Cities of India, rpt.Delhi 1977

Foster, William. (ed.) Early Travels in India 1583-1619, new Delhi, 1921

Frishman, M. and Khan, M., The Mosque, London, 1994

Frykenberg, R.E.(ed.) Delhi Through the Ages: Essays in Urban History, Culture and Society, Delhi, 1986

Fuhrer and Smith E. The Sharqi Architecture of Jaunpur, Delhi, 1889

Gascoigne, B., The Great Moghuls, London, 1971

Gavin, Hambly., Cities of Mughal India, London, 1968

Goetz, H., 'The Qudsia Bagh at Delhi: Key to Late Mughal Architecture' Islamic Culture, 26/I, 1952

Grover, Satish., An Outline of Islamic Architecture, Bombay, 1972

Habib, Irfan., The Agrarian System of Mughal India (1556-1707), Bombay 1963

Habib, M. and Nizami, K.A. (eds) A Comprehensive History of India, vol. V- The Delhi Sultanate 1206-1526, New Delhi, 1970

Haig, Sir Wolsley., The Cambridge History of India, vol.III, Turks and Afghans, New Delhi 1965

Harle, J.C., The Art and Architecture of the Indian Sub-Continent, Penguin, Harmondsworth, 1986

Havell, E., Indian Architecture, London, 1927 Hand book of Agra and the Taj, rpt.Delhi, 1971

Hearn, G.R., The Seven Cities of Delhi, London, 1906

Heber, Bishop Reginald., Narrative of a journey through the Upper Provinces of India from Calcutta to Bombay, 1824-1825, 3 vols., London, 1828

Hillenbrand, Robert., Islamic Art and Architecture, London, 1999

Hussian, M.A., Agra Fort, New Delhi, 1956

Ikram, S.M., Muslim Civilization in India, Columbia, 1965

Jairazbhoy, R.A., An Outline of Islamic Architecture, Bombay, 1972 'Early Garden Palaces of the Great Mughals', Oriental Art, N.S.4, 1958 Kanbo, M. Salih., Amal-i-Salih, 3 vols., Lahore, 1967

Kanwar, H.I.S., 'Subterranean Chambers of the Taj Mahal', Islamic Culture, vol. XLVIII, No. I, 1974 'Harmonious Proportions of the Taj Mahal', Islamic Culture, vol.49, 1975 'The Site of the Taj Mahal', Islamic Culture, vol.49, 1975

Kaul, H.K., Historic Delhi: An Anthology, Delhi, 1985

Khan, A.N., 'The Tomb of Anarkali at Lahore, Journal of Central Asia, 3/I, 1980

Khan, Inayat., Shah Jahan Nama, Eng. Trans. A.R.Fuller, rev.and ed. Begley nd Desai, New Delhi, 1970

Khan, Sayyid Ahmad., Asar-as-Sanadid,trans. by R.Nath as Monuments of Delhi, New Delhi, 1979

Koch, Ebba., Mughal Architecture : An Outline of its History and Development, Munich, 1991 'The Lost Colonnade of Shah Jahan's Bath in the Red Fort of Agra" in The Burlington Magazine,cxxiv, 1982

Lal, K.S., History of the Khiljis, Bombay, 1967

Lear, Edward., Edward Lear's Indian Journal, ed. By Ray Murphy, London, 1953

Llewellyn -Jones, Rosie., A Fatal Friendship: The Nawabs, the British and the City of Lucknow, Delhi, 1985

Lowry, G.D., 'Humayun's Tomb: From, Function and Meaning in Early Mughal Architecture', Muqarnas, 4, 1987

Lewis, Bernard (ed.) The World of Islam, London, 1976

Majumdar, R.C.(ed.) The Mughal Empire,Bombay, 1971

Manucci, Niccolao., Storia de Mogor; or Mughal India, London, 1907

Michell, George., (ed.) Architecture of the Islamic World London, 1978 (ed.) The Islamic Heritage of Bengal, Unesco, 1987 (ed.) Masterpieces of the Deccan Sultanates, Marg, Bombay Vol.XXXVII, No.3 (ed.) Brick Temples of Bengal, Princeton, 1983

Michell, George and Zebrowski, Mark., The Architecture and Art of the Deccan Sultanates, Cambridge, 1999

Mirza, M.W., The Life and Works of Amir Khusro, rpt.Delhi, 1974

Morris, J., Stones of Empire, Oxford, 1983

Moynihan,Elizabeth B.,'The Lotus Garden: Palace of Zahir al-Din Muhammad Babur', Muqarnas 5,1988 Paradise as a Garden in Persia and Mughal India, London, 1982

Mundy,Peter., The Travels of Peter Mundy in Europe and Asia, 1608-1667, 2 vols., London, 1914

Naqvi, S.A.A., Humayn's Tomb and Adjacent Buildings, Delhi, 1946

Nath, R., Agra and its Monumental Glory, Bombay, Colour Decoration in Mughal Architecture, Bombay, 1970 The Immortal Taj Mahal, Bombay, 1972

Page, J.A., Guide to the Qutb. Delhi, Delhi, 1938 (ed.) Monuments of Delhi, 4 vols., rpt.1997

Pal,P. and Leoshko, Janice et all., Romance of the Taj Mahal, Lodon 1989

Patil, D.R., Mandu, New Delhi, 1982

Prasad, Beni., History of Jehangir, London, 1922

Punja, S., Great Monuments of India, Hong Kong, 1994
Renton-Denning, J., Delhi: the Imperial City, Bombay, 1911

Rizvi, S.A.A., Fatehpur Sikri, New Delhi, 1992

Rizvi, S.A.A., and Flynn, V.A.A., Fatehpur Sikri, Bombay, 1975

Roe, Sir Thomas., The Embassy of Sir Thomas Roe to India 1615-19, ed. William Foster, 1899, rev.ed.London, 1926

Rowland, Benjamin., Art and Architecture of India, Harmondswoth, 1967

Sahai, Surendra., Delhi, Agra, Jaipur, Delhi, 1997

Saksena, Banarsi Prasad, History of Shahjahan of Dilhi, Allahabad, 1932

Sanderson, G., A Guide to the Buildings and Gardens, Delhi Fort, Delhi, 1937

Sharma, Y.D., Delhi and its Neighbourhood, New Delhi, 1982

Sharp, H., Historic Delhi, Delhi, 1980

Shrimali, K.M., (ed.) Reason and Archaeology, Delhi, 1998

Soundara Rajan, K.V., Islam Builds in India: Cultural Study of Islamic Architecture, Delhi, 1983

Spear, Percival., History of India, Penguin, London, 1986

Srivastava, A.L., The Sultanate of Delhi, Agra, 1974

Stephen, Carr., Archaeological and Monumental Remains of Delhi, Simla, 1876

Stuart, C.M.Villiers., Gardens of the Great Mughals, London, 1913

Tadgell, C., The History of Architecture in India, London, 1990

Tavernier, J.B., Travels in India, 2 vols.rpt.New Delhi, 1977

Thapar, Romila., History of India, vol.I, London, 1986

Tillotson, G.H.R., Mughal India, N.Y.1990

Welch, S.C., The Art of Mughal India, N.Y.1963

Yazdani, G., Mandu: the City of Joy, Oxford, 1929